THIS WILD LIFE

HEROINES
in the
HISTORY
of
BOTANY
1650-1850

Lucretia Saville Weems

This Wild Life: Heroines in the History of Botany 1650 -1850
by Lucretia Saville Weems

Copyright © 2023 by Lucretia Saville Weems

Published by New Northwest Productions, Ashland, Oregon

Cover and interior design by BookSavvyStudio.com

Library of Congress Control Number: 2023909025
ISBN: 978-1-7369129-8-0

This book is dedicated to the countless women around
the globe whose names are unknown to us, and who
for millennia have engaged in furthering
human wisdom about plants.

CONTENTS

INTRODUCTION

DRIVING DOWN A SLEEPY STREET ON A HOT SUMMER DAY, a little bungalow caught my eye. Or, rather, the rose growing up the front of it caught my eye. The house was nothing special; the paint peeling, probably 1920s vintage. But that rose! It had been there a very long time, and it was award-worthy. Smothered in small, soft yellow blooms, it covered the entire front of the house and beyond.

Harison's Yellow Rose
Courtesy thegardendiary.com

By the next block I was lost in thought. Who had planted that rose, and when? Where had it come from? How many nurseries were there to choose from 100 years ago? Who supplied the nurseries? Were there five roses available? Fifty?

Some sleuthing identified that rose as Rosa 'Harison's Yellow.' Tucked into covered wagons, wrapped in a bit of earth and cloth and kept alive with rationed water, it had marked the way west like Hansel and Gretel's crumbs. Along the pioneer trail the rose had lent the comfort of the familiar as settlers made homes in strange, often hostile surroundings. Families planted it at their homesteads and gave cuttings to fellow travelers who were continuing on.

"There is no cure for curiosity," said Dorothy Parker. And down the rabbit hole I went. The store of myth, fable and poetry created around plants is formidable and well known. Keep going and the recorded historic tales of their travels surface. They chart the journeys of plants around the globe at the hands of their human devotees, and, in turn, the stories of those fascinating humans.

Much of plant migration occurred during a period that would come to be known in Europe as the Age of Discovery. Hunger for the new is as old as mankind, and with the proliferation of sea travel around the globe from the 1500s on, trade in the foreign, the unusual and the exotic began to explode. Information about the natural world in all its facets would pour into Europe at a fever pitch for several hundred years. Exposure to new and wondrous living things was growing exponentially. No formal scientific categories existed; the field was called simply natural history.

The close of the 16th century saw the Portuguese accede dominance of the seaways to the Dutch, who would hold a monopoly on the massive global spice trade for many years. But the British were hard on their heels, and there were abundant goods to be traded beyond spices. Many of these goods were vegetal in nature; even before China and Japan became accessible, a staggering number of plants crossed paths with seafaring Europeans for the first time.

A byproduct of the British Empire's focus on territorial conquest above all else was the era of plant exploration. Collecting specimens for patrons or for trade became a full-fledged career, and a regular component of sea voyages. Collectors were an interesting lot, as were those who commissioned their endeavors. Both possessed the vision and drive to chase the unknown.

By and large plant collectors were iconoclastic and heroic. One finds tales of men who braved earthquakes and floods, disease, even bouts as hostages in enemy camps in order to collect plants. A high number of plant hunters succumbed to dramatic, premature deaths. Swashbuckling feats of derring-do were the order of the day, with explorers regularly facing a host of dangers in seeking out natural treasure to collect, transport and deliver.

One day, researching the history of a plant, I came across a distinctly female name in a list of plant explorers. Astonished, I dug deeper. The more I looked, the more I found. These were women whose names I had never heard; women from a variety of backgrounds whose adventures and accomplishments were dazzling. Each was a true heroine. Uncovering the facts of their lives and contributions has been a phenomenal adventure in itself.

Pharaoh Hatshepsut 1507 BCE-1458 BCE "The First Great Woman in History of Whom We Are Informed"
J.H. Breasted
Courtesy the Metropolitan Museum

The first known plant expedition occurred long ago and far away, and as a matter of fact it began with a woman. Hatshepsut was Pharaoh of all Egypt, and although she was not history's only female Pharaoh, her rule was the longest and the most prosperous. In 1470 BCE she charged her royal fleet with an expedition to the land of Punt, present-day Somalia.

Hatshepsut was building a temple, and her intention was to replicate the gardens of the gods. As those gardens were known to be terraced with myrrh trees she determined to bring and plant those trees in Egypt. "Thus the temple was made a splendid myrrh garden for the god, though the energetic Queen was obliged to send to the end of the known world to do this for him," remarked Egyptologist James Breasted. The voyage entailed leaving the Nile by canals and traveling down the coast of the Red Sea, and required the Egyptian fleet to be redesigned for the journey. The expedition was a success: 31 live myrrh trees as well as ebony, ivory, and a panther returned to Egypt with the sailors.

Nur Jahan, The Light of the World c. 1840
Artist Unknown
Courtesy indianminiaturepaintings.co.uk

In the late 1600s a woman called Nur Jahan would, incredibly, come to rule the Mughal empire at its zenith. The mighty kingdom was generating over a quarter of the global gross domestic product, and it was said that as they stormed and conquered across the land, Mughals left gardens in their wake. Nur and her husband Jahangir embraced and elevated that tradition.

"It is astonishing to find how many of the Mughal gardens throughout India and Kashmir owe their inception to, or were directly inspired by, the taste and the love of natural scenery and flowers of this royal lady, who… shared the joyous art-loving traditions of 'her' Turki and Persian ancestors," wrote Constance Villiers-Stuart in her seminal 1913 publication, *Gardens of the Great Mughals*.

Shalimar Bagh
Courtesy tripsontrack.com

When the couple visited Kashmir, Nur fell in love with the land and the vegetation and chose it for the site of the summer palace. For over twenty years the entire court decamped by elephant over the snowy passes in spring, and it was in Kashmir that Nur found the spectacular blue lily, Nymphaea nouchali caerulea. On her return to India she took cuttings and cultivated it there successfully.

Nymphaea Nouchali Caerulea
Courtesy worldoffloweringplants.com

Nearly a hundred years earlier the Flemish Princess Marie de Brimeu had been busy corresponding with the great botanist Carolus Clusius, whom Maximilian II had appointed director of the Imperial Medical Garden in Vienna. Clusius, "Father of the Tulip," numbered the Princess among his closest friends and most valuable botanical colleagues. A portion of their exchange regarding botanical matters is preserved in 27 letters dating from the late 1500s, and thus we know they not only corresponded, she also advised to him on plants. Due to Marie's influence, Clusius obtained an appointment at the university in Leiden and there created the earliest formal botanical garden. For the first time, plants were sought and grown to study in their own right rather than in the traditional medicinal context.

During the reign of Queen Mary II, the Dutch East India Company was at its zenith. As a child Mary was tutored by Henry Compton whose garden at Fulham Palace was regarded as a "museum" of unusual and exotic plants and was the site of her wedding. Mary was seriously invested in the quest for and propagation of imported plants, and in developing new varieties of existing plants. Her interest in plants expanded the botanical component of Dutch maritime activity dramatically. King William revoked existing restrictions on the Dutch East India Company's transport of exotic plant materials while exiled in Holland and Mary sponsored a

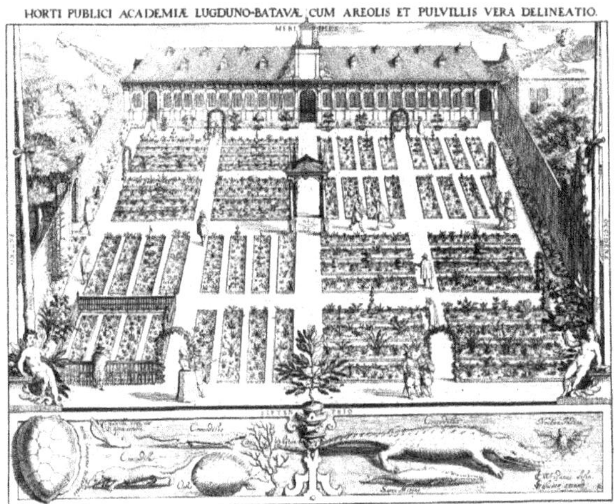

Clusius' Leiden Botanical Garden In 1610
Courtesy Collection Leiden University Libraries

wealth of seed-gathering expeditions. The palace gardens at Het Loo proudly displayed cactus, aloes, agaves and yuccas as well as orchids, and the blooms of trumpet vine and passionflowers draped the bowers with color.

As the years passed, more royal women lent their power to expanding the numbers of available plants for European gardens. They were passionate, knowledgeable and influential; naturally, fashion followed royal inclination.

Queen Charlotte, wife of King George III, would bring the tradition of the Christmas tree from Germany to England. Her biographer, Dr. John Watkins, paints the scene at a Christmas party in 1800: "In the middle of the room stood an immense tub with a yew tree placed in it, from the branches of which hung bunches of sweetmeats, almonds, and raisins in papers, fruits and toys, most tastefully arranged, and the whole illuminated by small wax candles. After the company had walked around and admired the tree, each child obtained a portion of the sweets which it bore together with a toy and then all returned home, quite delighted."

Charlotte was a gifted amateur botanist and trained her daughters as well. The King was terrifically supportive, as he was keen that his daughters never marry; in his fatherly wisdom he preferred they develop more rewarding interests and abilities. At Frogmore House, more recently the home of Meghan Markle and Prince Harry, the Queen created a serious botanical library and extensive plant collections in the gardens.

Fulham Palace
Courtesy Geographic Britain and Ireland

Charlotte's mother-in-law was Princess Augusta, who laid the foundation for Kew Gardens as we know it today. Augusta's friend the Earl of Bute was a plantsman who suggested she create a garden "containing all the plants on earth," an idea which piqued her delight. Charlotte would continue Augusta's work and it was to her the Earl of Bute dedicated his 12-volume publication on the plants of Great Britain, *Botanical Tables*.

"You're interested in botany?" wrote Napoleon to Joseph Banks in 1804. "So is my wife." The Empress Josephine wanted to create "the most beautiful and curious garden in Europe." She sponsored plant expeditions around the globe, importing and experimenting with naturalizing eucalyptus, lilies and over fifty varieties of geranium. The number of roses in cultivation in France exploded due to her sponsorship. While England and France were at war, British ships carrying plants destined for her gardens were allowed to pass unhindered. One English nurseryman was issued a special passport to guarantee his goods arrived in prime condition. At the Empress's estate, Chateau Malmaison, zebras, black swans, llamas, kangaroos and gazelles roamed freely on warm nights in the gardens. Like its mistress, Malmaison had a brief but spectacular reign as the crown jewel of the French landscape.

To you leading ladies of bygone days, we gratefully bow. You lent your power and vision to the world of plants, and through your passion, patronage and gardens you shepherded the field of botany into being.

PROLOGUE

THE WORLD WAS A VERY DIFFERENT PLACE as this story begins. In 1676 in England, boring a hole in a tree and filling it with honey was the traditional way to produce sweet fruit. Plants were watered with colored water to produce the desired color of flowers. Spontaneous generation—the idea that non-living objects could give rise to life forms—was the prevailing theory of life. Take as evidence the frogs that appeared on the banks of the Nile every spring out nowhere, or the mice that appeared when a piece of cheese or bread was left wrapped in a damp cloth for a while. Not until Louis Pasteur's work in 1859 was that idea put to rest.

In England a woman was not allowed to attend university or to vote. The careers of doctor, lawyer, professor were fully closed to women. The Witchcraft Act, making it a crime to accuse a person of magical powers or witchcraft, did not become the law until 1735. The Royal Society, that bastion of knowledge founded in 1662, would not allow women in its membership until 1945.

These are the stories of seven women and their work in the world of plants over a two hundred year period, roughly 1650-1850. All of them are anglo-European. The five who engaged in natural history research in foreign lands were able to travel as a result of Empire, that dubious host. By the late 1600s Dutch dominance of global sea trade was ending and the British presence rising. The women who explored in India, South America, Ceylon, Madeira, Tenerife and South Africa were—at least initially—accompanying husbands or fathers in the military. In Sarah Bowdich Lee's case, the Royal Africa Company briefly employed her husband, which occasioned their first trip to West Africa.

Two of the women contributed mightily to the coming field of botany by creating repositories of learning: Mary Somerset through her prodigious plant cultivation and documentation, and Margaret Bentinck through her powerful informal laboratory at Bulstrode, her country home. They were both women of means, and they devoted those means wholeheartedly to the development of knowledge in the world of plants and the natural sciences.

Finding source data for women in science during this period is a true quest. We know that historically and on each continent the indigenous informants regarding the plant kingdom have been largely female. And yet, most of the female names I unearthed were accompanied with next to no detail. Although the women in these pages represent a very small group, I am grateful that luck and opportunity enabled their heroic adventures, and that the records allowed their stories to be passed on for the modern reader. No strangers to bias and marginalization, each of them would wholeheartedly applaud the current work to honor indigenous involvement in plant exploration, and acknowledgement of the terribly skewed lens through which plant exploration has been seen, documented and named.

I.

SANITY

Mary Somerset
Duchess of Beaufort
1630-1715

Mary Somerset, Duchess of Beaufort
from Mary Capel and her Sister Elizabeth
by Sir Peter Lely c.1670
Courtesy Metropolitan Museum

ON A CHILLY GLOUCESTERSHIRE MORNING a woman rises early, wraps herself tightly in a shawl, and begins the long walk through her house. Down the stairs, past the Billiard Room, the Duke's Sitting Room, the Red Room with its family portraits, the Library. Into the South Wing, through the massive kitchens and out the door. She crosses to an adjoining building.

This building has an unusual amount of glass but even more unusual is the temperature. A large stove is being stoked by three men, and the thermometer reads 80 degrees. Shelves throughout the large room match the heat in color, filled with the hues of the tropics.

The year is 1696, the place is Mary Capel Somerset's hothouse, and each of the shelves is filled with plants imported from the far corners of the globe, growing for the first time in Europe.

Word has come that a long-awaited shipment will be arriving today, and from her window this morning she spotted an ox-drawn cart in the distance. The cart is filled with bathtub-like containers; in the tubs, trees. A man named James Weir dug the plants four months earlier in Barbados, where he awaited passage for Mary's cargo on a vessel bound directly for London.

As the cart rattles through the massive ironwork gates, the boy sitting alongside the driver turns and says: "We're there now, Pa?" "Two, three mile more, son. We're at Badminton, but the house is a ways yet."

Badminton was the home of Mary and her second husband, Henry Somerset. Indeed, the approach to Badminton House consisted of an avenue two-and-a-half miles long and two hundred feet wide, flanked by adjoining eighty-foot-wide avenues on either side. The grounds were designed as a Copernican view of the heavens with Badminton House as the earth, exerting its gravitational pull on all the heavenly bodies via numerous paths. From the house itself a dozen avenues radiated, many of them miles long. The estate spanned over 900 acres and its splendor was said to rival that of Versailles. Because of the Duke's wife, Mary Somerset, Duchess of Beaufort, Badminton was also the site of tremendous achievements in the formative days of botany.

The tall woman who greeted the cart was no longer young. Mary's youth had been tumultuous, as she came from a family of Royalists, and the English Civil war was at its height. Both her first husband, Henry Seymour, and her father were imprisoned in London Tower, and by the time she was 24 her father had been hanged and Henry had slit his own throat.

Mary's life as a widow was miserable. Unwanted, she was under the thumb of the Seymour family both financially and emotionally. An intelligent and spirited young woman, Mary was stunned at her utter loss of sovereignty. Enter Henry Somerset, a handsome, bright and brash Welshman. He must have seen in Mary a capable partner equally motivated to restore her rightful place in England: Somerset was promised in marriage to Princess Elizabeth but the war had put an end to the match. He proposed to Mary, and with only the support of her mother, she accepted and remarried at the age of 29.

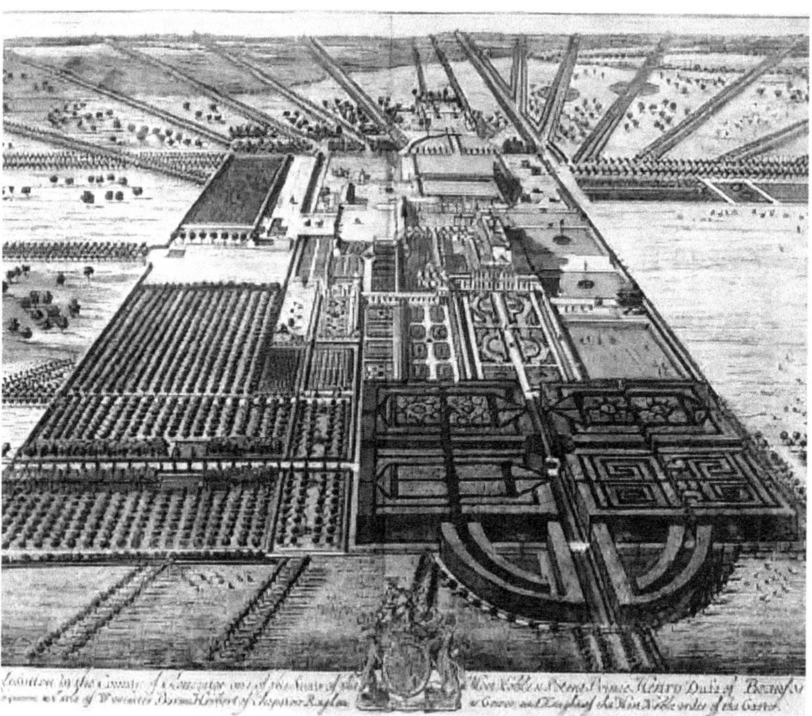

Badminton House 1709 Johannes Kip, Leonard Knyff
Courtesy Abe Books

The two prospered, and soon Badminton was their home. History has it that Mary and Henry were joined by ambition, but their marriage was certainly built on mutual respect and devotion, if not classical romantic love. Early on, Henry expresses hopes in a letter that "my great affection for you may a little supply the want of my person." On acquiring Badminton, Henry looked to Mary completely for its management. He trained her in keeping the accounts, and she was a quick study.

Like many grand country houses it functioned like a small village, employing some 200 people to keep the wheels turning. Beer, candles and soap were all made on site. Mary was an exacting employer and made full rounds of the entire estate daily. She also served as Henry's representative for the neighboring garrison under his command. More than once she was required to step in and manage political emergencies. She tried her hand in local politics as well but found it singularly unrewarding.

Despite her competence and position, Mary carried a personal weight: a cyclical, paralyzing depression. Whether the source was biological or the result of her early griefs, the effects were concerning to husband and friends. "Have as great a care for your own health as it is possible, and banish what you can of all melancholy apprehensions," pleads Henry. Her neighbor, Lady Chaworth, wrote to a mutual friend, "She has gone almost into a mopishness with melancholy." Although it came and went, her condition was intensifying as the years progressed. By 1675, Mary was at a nadir, with neither appetite nor the heart for her household obligations, bookkeeping or even letter writing. Keeping down a meal became a challenge.

An advisor surfaced. The theologian Joseph Glanvil was a founding member of the Royal Society and a family friend. Several of his widely published books were dedicated to the Somerset family and he was often in attendance at Badminton. An unusual combination of qualities, Glanvill was a devout Anglican, yet a philosophical skeptic and staunch supporter of free thought. He was remarkably prescient, claiming that one day man would go to the moon and magnetic waves would connect people across the globe.

Glanvill's philosophy held that the quality of melancholy allowed for the entry of unfortunate spirits into one's person, and that pursuit of scientific inquiry and rational analysis of the natural world was the remedy. The idea spoke to Mary and it opened the door to her life's work. Over time, and to the great good fortune of botany, she turned more and more to her gardens for healing and respite.

Mary's initial interest in plants and gardening was personal and medicinal; she sought knowledge of herbal remedies to treat her emotional imbalances. But she was also a duchess, and Beaufort House, her London home in Chelsea, was the site of grand events. It was there that Mary started forming relationships with the leading gardeners, nurserymen and florists of the time. She began cultivating auriculas, polyanthus, peonies and carnations in grand seasonal displays. Massive flower gardens were installed below the terraces, and huge beds of anemone, jonquil, tulip and fritillaria were planted for spring show.

It was a very exciting time to be in London if you loved plants. In 1681 George London and Henry Wise opened Brompton Park Nursery, which truly transformed the possibilities of gardening in England. Brompton Park was the first large-scale nursery in Europe, and any one plant was available into the thousands. Located on land now occupied by the Victoria and Albert Museum, it covered over 50 acres. The total supply of stock was estimated at several million plants. George London had been gardener to Mary's brother at Casiobury, their family estate, and to Bishop Compton and his renowned gardens at Fulham Palace. Soon he was assisting the Duchess at Beaufort House. In 1684, Charles II attended festivities there and lavished his hosts with royal approbation.

Surely kismet adjoined Beaufort House to the Chelsea Physic Garden. There, Hans Sloane, doctor to the royal family and to Mary, reigned over his own botanical realm. He had studied at Chelsea Physic in his youth and bought the property in 1680. The friendship between Mary and Sloane would be long and productive. They collaborated mightily on plant introductions, and their work marked an era of transition in England from plants studied in a chiefly medicinal context to the birth of botany in its own right.

Chelsea Physic Garden.
Plan View Engraving by John Haynes 1751
Courtesy Wellcome Collection

Sloane's reputation as a doctor was vague. Many dismissed him as a society doctor, specializing in the skills of interacting with important people above excellence in medicine. But he was a terrifically curious man. His zealous interest in natural history and particularly in plants was lifelong. Judging from the collections he amassed, study of the natural world was his passion.

The Temple Coffee House Botany Club was Britain's first natural history organization, and it is said to have started because of Hans Sloane. Sloane's presence had been requested in Jamaica to serve as the governor's physician. When Mary heard of the appointment she stepped in, sponsoring Sloane to include plant collecting as part of his duties. He returned from his tenure in the tropics with a bounty of specimens and stories to share with his fellow botanists: He had amassed over 800 new plant introductions to Europe during his time on the island!

The era of the coffee house was in full swing in London on Sloane's return. The height of fashion, these establishments' popularity mark a moment when the relentless pulse of Empire skipped a beat; rank and class distinctions were magically put aside, and men from every walk of life gathered to discuss business and politics, sharing all manner of information. A visiting Prussian count noted it was "a Sort of Rule with the English, to go once a Day at least" to coffee-houses "where they talk of Business and News, read the Papers, and often look at one another." Information and ideas were the commodities, and different coffee houses catered to different interests. Lawyers, artists, travelers and the clergy all had their favorite. Some drew the literati, while some had brothels attached. Others hosted the conversations that birthed the stock exchange and the insurance industry, the latter in an establishment called Lloyd's.

Of a Friday evening, the leading lights of the British plant world crowded into the front room at the Temple Coffee House: William Sherard, John Ray, the Bobarts father and son, who headed the Oxford Physic Garden, Philip Miller and the colorful James Petiver were there, along with Sloane. We will encounter each of them again. Merchants, sea captains and adventurers returning from foreign lands joined as well, exchanging information and theories about plants with Royal Society fellows. It will come as no surprise women were by and large unwelcome in coffee houses. Though she was a highly respected collegue, the Duchess did not attend these all-male gatherings.

At Badminton, Mary had begun growing oranges. Oranges were the first plants to defy zone-ism in Britain through the introduction of simple greenhouses, or orangeries. These buildings had plentiful and unusually large windows, and a stove or open fire for heat. In Amsterdam, the next iteration was in development. There the entire floor of the building was plumbed for hot air via charcoal braziers. Mary would be among the first in England to convert her greenhouse to a hothouse.

Mary Somerset's Orangerie Today
Courtesy DiCamillo Travel

With that innovation, Badminton became the place where literally thousands of plants were grown and catalogued in Europe for the first time. Mary embarked on research in naturalizing new plants coming to England from tropical locales around the globe. Her initial interest in herbal medicine, or *simpling* as it was then called, was evolving into serious botanical expertise. She was determined, intelligent and terribly talented.

Her ability to raise an imported seed was unmatched. She grew the first zonal and ivy-leaved pelargoniums in England, as well as aloes, bananas, nerine, pawpaw, hibiscus, guava, arum lilies and mesembryanthemums. The first passiflora caerulea in Europe bloomed in her gardens.

When Sloane saw his Jamaica introductions in her gardens, he said, "I never saw West India plants in such perfect condition out of their own climate as there. The Plants themselves have been likewise brought over, planted, and throve very well…where they are not only rais'd some few handfuls high, but come to Perfection, flower and produce their ripe

Fruits, even to my Admiration; and that, by the Direction of her Grace the Duchess of Beaufort, who at her leisure Hours, from her more serious Affairs, has taken pleasure to command the raising of Plants in her Garden, where, by means of Stoves and Infirmaries, many of them have come to greater Perfection, than in any Part of Europe."

William Sherard, second only to John Ray in botanical stature, was a serious fan. He tutored Mary in plant taxonomy as she made the transition from talented gardener to botanist. He would come to live at Badminton, serving as overseer of her greenhouses and botany tutor for the children.

Jacob Bobart followed Mary's progress as well. In a letter to her, he notes the "glorious success of your plantations, grown under the auspicious supervising of such a patroness who daily makes appear the transcendent wealth of the Vegetable Kingdom."

The great parson naturalist John Ray, to whom the term "species" is credited, worked with Mary identifying and classifying tropical plant samples from many sources over the years. Ray further honored her in requesting the use of her herbarium in his development of taxonomy for tropical flora.

Soon Mary was growing seed from Portugal, the Canary Islands, Sri Lanka, Japan and Africa. Bishop Compton supplied her with North American seeds via John Banister, as did the Byrd family and the Governor of Virginia. Sloane sent plants from Switzerland. George London was already sharing seeds with Mary and the Bishop from China and the West Indies, and Sherard also supplied Chinese seeds. Mary's brother Harry contributed seeds from India, and Mary regularly sent seeds and cuttings to friends in the colonies as well.

The more plants she grew, the more passionate she became to obtain those she knew of but did not have. A letter from Jacob Bobart to Somerset's gardener, Mr. Adams, in 1695/6 says: "I have sent all those Plants wch Her Grace was pleased to express Her desire of viz. / The Perfuming Chery of Arabia / White Barberry / Cornus Americana folio serrato / Ribes Grossularie folio / Sambucus racemosa fructu rubio / Laburnum majus / And an excellent plant of my jewell of a Primrose (and 12 sorts of all the best Roses)."

Further, Mary understood what it took to successfully prepare specimens for a long ocean voyage: "If some small plants that have roots be taken up wth a considerable part of the root (and each root wrap't round wth some of the most clayy earth that country affords), & put into a chest or box, the empty part fill'd wth mosse or some such sort of thing, it is hope'd they may come into England from thence, wth as good suces as Orreng lemon &c does out of Italy, which many times, since the warr's, have laien 3 moneths in chests & yet growne very well."

Plant transport was a tremendous challenge in the first days of seafaring botanical collection. Casualties of specimens were plentiful. The solution would not come for several decades, with the invention of the first simple terrarium, the Wardian Case, in 1830. More about that and its inaugural users anon.

The botanical gadfly, James Petiver, also found Mary's plants "raised to a perfection I never saw before." He would link Mary to the work of the amazing Maria Sibylla Merian.

A tremendous character in his own right, Petiver was one of the few non-gentlemen, non-doctors of the Temple House group. With his boundless enthusiasm and determination to have a finger in every pie, he served the natural sciences very well. An apothecary by profession, life at his shop was a constant flurry of activity, if not mayhem.

The address of his shop was "familiar to brother apothecaries, shipmasters, merchants, planters, physicians, surgeons, ministers of the gospel, consuls, ambassadors, privy councilors, peers of the realm, and foreign gentlemen of various degrees extending from Moscow to the Cape of Good Hope and from the British Colonies in the New World to the Spanish settlements in the Philippines. From this shop were dispatched thousands of letters and queries, occasional bits of medical advice together with shipments of drugs and nostrums, newssheets, scientific pamphlets and books, frequent consignments of brown paper, wide-mouthed bottles, and detailed instructions for amateur naturalists and collectors who had set forth—or were on the point of setting forth—to nearby English counties or to far-off foreign lands."

Petiver was relentless in courting new agents and collectors, and took great pride in his recruiting style. Here, a note requesting a meeting with a Mr. Evans in 1697: "Kind Friend: With noe less ardent desire am I possest to see the Shells you promist, then passionate Lover waits for Night or ye sooner appointed hour of his charming Mistress."

Although collecting natural history specimens was becoming a plausible career, it was not stress-free. One Jezreel Jones wrote to Petiver from Cadiz: "The place I am in is in great confusion and the Spaniards are so ill natured upon the rumours of a warr that a Stranger, especially an English [-man], can not tell how to please them; I have been suspected for one that Studys witchcraft, Necromancy, and a Madman by some who observed me following butterflies, picking of herbs and other lawful exercises and I have had much to do to escape the censure of the higher powers."

Maria Sibylla Merian Plate I
Metamorphosis Insectorum Surinamensium
Courtesy Lloyd Library and Museum

Petiver set out to Amsterdam on a collecting expedition in 1703. He made a point to meet Maria Sibylla Merian. Several years prior to that meeting, Merian had returned from an unprecedented expedition to Surinam to study and record butterflies and other insects in their habitats. Well into her fifties and accompanied only by her daughter, she had spent two years in the harsh and utterly wild tropical environment. The work she published on her return, *Metamorphosis Insectorum Surinamensium*, would become a seminal contribution to entomology, botany and ecology. It contained 60 spectacular paintings of plants and insects unknown outside of the tropics. Merian was fascinated with metamorphosis, and was the first person to study and record it in detail. Before her work, spontaneous generation was still the prevailing theory! An entire genus of plants and two genera are named after Merian, as well as a lizard, a toad, a lily, a snail, a bird, and several butterflies and spiders

Despite the fact that the Dutch were by and large unimpressed by Petiver (apparently his Latin was awful, and his hygiene sporadic), Merian enlisted his help in selling subscriptions in London for *Insectorum Surinamensium*. Petiver loyally presented on her behalf at the Royal Society for years following their meeting.

And thus *Metamorphosis Insectorum Surinamensium* found its way into Mary Somerset's library. The insects in her own garden had not escaped her notice. She commented to Richard Bradley she believed every species of butterfly and moth has its own food, an observation no one in England had made. She also tried her hand at butterfly breeding. She was an excellent needlewoman and studied butterflies to create patterns for her embroidery work. In this, too, Merian's paintings were invaluable.

Mary Somerset and Maria Merian pioneered a dramatic detour from the prevailing fashion, laying the foundations for the ecological systems approach of the distant future. Dried specimens and their classification were the focus of men in both botany and entomology. Despite the numerous methods used for classification in this pre-Linnaean period, both of these women were able to record an astonishing amount of data that accurately reflected living things. Both were interested in the life of their subjects, their growth and habits; and they collected, organized, and recorded information within that context for the first time.

When Mary's husband died in 1700, botany took center stage in the Duchess' life. Dogged curiosity and intelligence drove her to move beyond a prodigious talent at cultivation. She steeped herself in research. With plant taxonomy having no one dominant system, there was a great range of sources for classification, making cross-referencing vital when placing plants in their proper context. Much of Mary's correspondence and notes focused on categorizing plants and, based on her personal observation, accurately correcting existing published data.

Mary had grown up with gardens as a way of life. Her mother was Elizabeth Morrison, whose family estate at Chipping Campden boasted eight acres of gardens. Her father's family estate, Hadham Hall, was built for a bishop in the 11th century, coming into the Capel family in the 1400s. Its well-known garden was Italianate in design, with fountains, statuary, and terraces for viewing the deer park and woods.

The Capel Family, Cornelis Johnson c.1640
Courtesy National Portrait Gallery

Mary is shown as a young girl in a Capel family portrait. The prescient painter placed her directly in the foreground of the family gardens. Her sister Elizabeth, who would become a renowned flower artist, was painted handing her sister a rose. Mary's two brothers would also create and tend serious gardens as adults: Henry Capel collected and gardened at Kew, his wife's property, laying the groundwork there for the future Royal Botanical Gardens. According to John Evelyn, Henry grew "the choicest fruit of any in England." Arthur Capel developed the extensive gardens at Casiobury, the Capel family estate, which boasted an avenue of 295 lime trees. Each of the Capel children embraced the remarkable legacy of gardens and plants they were given, made it their own, and built on it.

The same did not hold true for Mary's children. Through her botanical pursuits, she had vanquished her inner struggles. Yet in the relationships with her children and grandchildren a personal connection was somehow lacking. She had been tenacious in representing their holdings throughout her life, fighting on their behalf whenever the opportunity of enlarging their various estates presented itself. Nonetheless, each found fault with her and accused her of self-interest.

At the height of Badminton House's glory Mary wrote that, in many ways, she felt the trials of success and its attendant responsibilities as keenly as she had felt those of her disfavored widowhood. She could not then know that there was more pain in store: At 80 years of age, she was forced out of Badminton by her grandson.

Mary passed her final days at Beaufort House in London. She commissioned Everhard Kick to create paintings for a florilegium of her finest botanical blooms in two volumes, which remains in the library at Badminton. She personally created a 12-volume herbarium under Sloane's encouragement and expressed regret she had not made it bigger, as she had many more volumes' worth of specimens yet to add! This she bequeathed to Sloane. It accompanied the rest of his personal collections in the founding of the British Museum.

She acquired an impressive amount of source material in order to feed her hunger for taxonomy, cataloguing accurately each and every last addition to her gardens and greenhouses. Her aim was to have every species of every plant represented, and indeed the breadth of plants at Badminton was that of a true botanical garden. She writes apologetically to Sloane, "When I get into storys of plants I know not how to get out."

After her death, Stephen Switzer, the renowned garden designer who started his career at Brompton Court Nursery, visited Badminton. In his publication, *Ichnographia Rustica*, he writes of Mary, "It would be an unpardonable omission not to mention those virtuous and honorable persons among the ladies who have likewise shewn particular Veneration and Esteem for the subject we are upon…the great favor she held towards virtuosos in her own way I have in several great instances heard."

Modern Day Badminton
Courtesy habituallychic.luxury

Badminton remains in the Beaufort family to this day. Canaletto painted it several times under the patronage of the fourth Duke. Queen Elizabeth lived there for much of World War II. In the 1940s, it became the site of the Badminton Horse Trials. The 11th Duke of Beaufort recently died there, leaving a $325 million pound fortune.

The gardens are open to the public each year, and one can even go home with a plant grown there. But the achievement, innovation and discovery generated by one extraordinary woman over three hundred years ago remain the pinnacle of accomplishment at Badminton.

The genus Beaufortia, comprised of twenty-two species, was named in homage to her in 1914. Mary Somerset's formidable contributions met with slim recognition. Yet she brought a truly heroic level of innovation, research and documentation to the world of botany. All of us who garden stand gratefully on her shoulders.

Beaufortia Splendens, Jean Jules Linden 1854
One of 22 Species In The Genus
Courtesy finerareprints.com

II.

SCANDAL

Lady Anne Monson
1726-1776

Bombax Ceiba Linn

Arum Esculentum

"Paper Mosaicks," Mary Delany
After Drawings by Lady Anne Monson in Madras
Courtesy British Museum

Poor Charles. Lady Anne, his wife, was the talk of the town. Charles had taken leave of the family and his seat in Parliament to tour the Continent at the age of 44. He chose the fashionable architect Robert Adam as his travel companion, and the two set off for Pisa to join Charles' older son, who was being tutored there. The two men fell out; Adam was replaced with a minor Scottish art dealer, and on went Charles.

Charles Hope-Vere steeped himself in art and architecture for over a year. Feeling confident his connoisseurship had ascended to a sufficiently lofty new pinnacle, he returned home, where an unexpected development greeted him: His and Lady Anne's two sons had a new sibling. He filed for divorce, a very unusual procedure that required an act of Parliament in 1757. It was granted.

Perhaps heritage had a hand. Lady Anne was not the first in her family to display a lack of respect for the institution of marriage. Her aunt Anne was mistress to George II. Her great-grandfather was the Merrie Monarch Charles II, famous for a reign of debauch, to wit Lady Anne's great-grandmother Barbara Villiers. Villiers was easily the king's most illustrious mistress and cut a very wide swath at Court in her day. She was a legendary beauty; mercurial, with a quick wit and a quicker temper, she was known equally for acts of ruthlessness and kindness. Of an evening she would consistently be found at the gaming table, with the King as her banker. Her long string of lovers was not limited to the King nor even to gentlemen of the Court, but included circus performers, actors and—horrors—playwrights. John Evelyn detested her; Samuel Pepys was somewhat shamefacedly in her thrall.

In the event, divorce finalized, Lady Anne Hope-Vere departed life at court with aplomb, never looking back. She left her children behind, married again, and went on to historic achievements. Society predictably sided mostly with Charles, but Charles' erstwhile companion Robert Adam understood Lady Anne. He described Charles Hope-Vere as a "poor, vain, childish coxcomb."

Happily for us Lady Anne took along her lifelong fascination with botany when she departed. Her London home became a well-known gathering place for English naturalists, in particular followers of the great Swedish natural scientist Linnaeus. Linnaeus' method of taxonomy, the classification of living things, was gaining momentum. Its adoption would dramatically and permanently shape scientific endeavor, and Lady Anne, alongside her friend James Lee, played a major role in that historic shift.

Lee was a Scot, who had walked from Aberdeen to London in his youth and landed an apprenticeship at Chelsea Physic Garden, where Philip Miller was busy creating an herbarium of plants from all over the world. In 1745 Lee founded Vineyard Nursery in Hammersmith with William Kennedy. "For many years," wrote John Claudius Loudon 100 years later, "this nursery was deservedly considered the first in the world," first in the sense of pre-eminent. "His extensive stoves greenhouse and nursery was the emporium of all that was curious and interesting in Botany."

Lee met Linnaeus when the Swede visited Chelsea Physic Gardens, exchanging and identifying plant samples with Miller and his staff. Linnaeus and Lee corresponded from that point on, as Lee was enthusiastic about adopting Linnaeus' new taxonomic system.

Lady Anne was a believer as well, certain the Linnaean system was the future. She persuaded Lee to undertake with her the translation of Linnaeus' introductory work, *Philosophia Botanica Naturae*, from Latin into English. She had the Latin he lacked, and each had a thorough understanding of the botanical realm. *Introduction to Botany; Extracted from the Works of Dr. Linnaeus* was published in 1760.

"Such neatness! Such beauty! More easy for beginners!" declared the felicitously named botanist Alexander Garden, writing from South Carolina. The public agreed wholeheartedly. Suddenly there was a simple system for plant identification. Overnight one need not rely on numerous reference books written in Latin to step into the world of plant collecting, observing and identifying. What had been a jumble of taxonomic systems, intertwining and overlapping randomly, had been streamlined by Linnaeus.

In his approach, classification and naming of organisms brought together botanical thought and biology. To his system we owe the prime identification mainstays of today: animal, vegetable and mineral. With

Linnaeus' work translated into English, knowledge of Latin became unimportant. Interest and developments in botany exploded throughout the English-speaking world.

The work was published under Lee's name, and his acknowledgement in the printed volume is to an anonymous friend. It was at Lady Anne's insistence that she remained anonymous. She had had her fill of scandal. Astonishingly, she full well knew that had her name appeared in print, the uproar would have surpassed that caused by bearing a child not her husband's. Women—and certainly nobility—simply did not publish.

Sir James Smith, founder of the Linnaean Society, acknowledged it was indeed Lady Anne to whom Lee referred, and that she was the driving force behind the work. The publication went to ten editions. Even the skeptical Philip Miller came around to her thinking. Granted, his famous *Gardeners Dictionary* was in its 8th edition before he began acknowledging and incorporating the Linnaean system.

Both Lady Anne and James Lee were friends of Joseph Banks, whose own botanical star was on the rise. One evening over dinner at Lady Anne's home, Linnaeus' star pupil, Daniel Solander, leapt to his feet on hearing Banks announce the confirmation of his *Endeavour* voyage with Captain Cook. Solander enthusiastically offered to join the expedition. "Someone like you would be a constant benefit and pleasure to me!" said Banks. Thus began that historic collaboration. It would be to Lee's Hammersmith's Vineyards Nursery that Banks took the collected plant cuttings from the returned *Endeavour* voyage for propagation.

From Sweden, Linnaeus was actively sending his students forth to proselytize and to collect. One of the Swedish botanists who found a welcome at Lady Anne's was Clas Alstromer. In 1764, he wrote to Linnaeus of Lady Anne: "She has made more progress in botanical science than any other woman, not superficially…but in a close and profound way".

Alstromer told Linnaeus what a pleasure it would be for Lady Anne to have a plant named in her honor. "She deserves it, and it should encourage her to sacrifice life and property to Science," said Alstomer. He went so far as to compare Lady Anne's botanical learning with that of the formidable Duchess of Portland, with the Duchess coming out very unfavorably.

He also mentioned that at Lady Anne's table, each dinner commenced with a toast to Linnaeus. Perhaps Alstromer's tidbits inspired Linnaeus' torrid letter to Lady Anne, whom he had never met. He stewed for some years, and then wrote: "I have never seen your face, but in my sleep I often dream of you. If you love me too, can I join you in the procreation of just one little daughter to bear witness of our love—a little Monsonia, through which your fame would live forever in the Kingdom of Flora."

Cape of Good Hope c. 1731 by Scott And Lambert
Courtesy British Library

The naming in fact occurred, though it would be some years later, after Lady Anne's visit to Monsonia's native land. Colonel George Monson, her second husband, was a distinguished career military man and was posted to Calcutta in 1774.

Lady Anne set out to join him and to experience the botanical splendor of the tropics. Putting in at the Cape of Good Hope for fresh supplies was the custom of eastbound Indiaman ships, and there she found excellent botanical companionship. Francis Masson and Carl Thunberg were in residence. Masson, a close friend of James Lee, was collecting for Joseph Banks on behalf of Kew. Thunberg, a Swede, was a Linnaean apostle collecting en route to Japan. Lady Anne arrived with her personal draftsman, and the four undertook several botanical expeditions together. After her departure the two men sent to Linnaeus the lovely plant which was named after her.

On her arrival in Calcutta Lady Anne continued to botanize, and to draw the plants of India. Mary Delany, the Duchess of Portland's great friend, would use several of those drawings in creating her remarkable "paper Mosaicks." Lady Anne also assembled a fabulous collection of insect specimens that she sent to James Lee's daughter in London.

Her reputation as a hostess of wit and charm had preceded her arrival in India, and she did not disappoint. For one, she was a wizard at the card table. Her remarkable skills at whist have found their way into more than one historian's account of colonial life in Calcutta. She was a favorite of Sir Philip Francis, who loved cards, and in fact amassed a tremendous fortune through his winnings in the East Indies. Francis would return from India to a seat in Parliament and a peerage; in Calcutta, however, he distinguished himself differently. At his mistress' house one evening while her husband was away, the lady's servants noticed a ladder in the garden, and on the ladder a man ascending to their mistress' bedchamber window. They promptly hauled Francis down and tied him up for the night. The lady in question was Madame Grand, the famous beauty who left India to become the de facto second lady of France as Talleyrand's mistress.

In Calcutta, Francis and Colonel Monson allied in an effort to bring down Warren Hastings, the first Governor General of India. The era of the Nabob was in full flower, with many an Englishman, including high ranking military men, returning from India flaunting huge and questionably gained fortunes as a result of the British East India Company's operations, which more resembled a government than a business. The political climate was ripe for a scapegoat, and Francis had a personal score to settle. After Hastings commented publicly on Francis' lack of moral propriety, Francis challenged the Governor General to a duel, but emerged the loser.

How Monson came to side with Francis is unknown. But clearly a trace of bitterness surfaced in Lady Anne as well, perhaps the remains of her banishment at court. Her botanical interests were put aside as she turned her substantial influence to decrying Hastings, spreading tawdry tales of his origins, which were patently false. "Even if she believed what was so untrue, spiteful gossip of the kind came doubly badly from Lady Anne Monson. Her own young days had been saddened by a romance of folly and sorrow which if it had not taught her the charity which is kind should have at least suggested to her the unwisdom of throwing stones," said Dr. W.E. Busteed in his memoir, *Echoes of Old Calcutta.*

South Park Street Cemetery, Calcutta

Lady Anne's Headstone
at the Cemetery
Courtesy India Times blog 2012

Francis and Monson brought multiple charges against Hastings, forcing him to return to London and stand trial. After an expensive court battle lasting eight years, Hastings was fully acquitted. A serious gardener, he retired to his family home in England, and spent his post-India years gardening in the style he had begun in India, combining tropical plants with beloved English standards.

Hastings would outlive both Colonel and Lady Monson by quite a few years. As with many Europeans before them, the extreme nature of the tropical climate was the undoing of the Monsons. Lady Anne died after two years in India, and the Colonel several years later. In the British Library, Lady Anne is kindly and rightfully remembered foremost as a "learned lady botanist of her time".

Monsonia lobata, L'Herbier General 1 1816 by Pancrace Bessa
The genus Monsonia consists of 39 species.
Courtesy worthpoint.com

III.

BOUNTY

Margaret Bentinck
Duchess of Portland
1715-1785

Margaret Cavendish Holles-Harley 1738
Christian Zincke
Courtesy harleygallery.co.uk

THE SCIENTISTS WERE DAZZLED. Gathered in a field outside of London to view the total solar eclipse, they had witnessed a sight of ethereal beauty. Flashes of light sparkling at the edges of the moon formed a brilliant halo around the black disc just as totality approached. It was caused by sunlight passing through the canyons of the moon.

The astronomer Edmund Halley was the host. The year was 1715, and he named the phenomenon Baily's Beads. For his next undertaking Halley intended to calculate the distance of the Earth from the sun, and to do so he needed to map the transit of Venus.

The Royal Society rallied around the idea and mobilized an effort to that end in 1761, recruiting 120 people from nine nations. The weather did not cooperate, and it was a failure. In 1769, they redoubled their efforts and sent Captain Cook to Tahiti, the location thought to be ideal for observing and recording the transit. An ambitious young man named Joseph Banks talked his way into joining the expedition. He knew there was a second, secret agenda: The search for a rumored Southern Continent. His interest was natural history, and he was willing to underwrite a lavish contingent whose mission would be to explore and collect the flora and fauna of all the distant islands encountered on the expedition.

The continent that came to be known as Australia was indeed found and mapped. Banks returned to England a hero, due to the remarkable number of natural history specimens he brought back. In plants alone, Banks and his companion, Daniel Solander, returned with over 500 varieties unknown in Europe. His success created the momentum to support the beginnings of the Royal Botanic Gardens at Kew—with Banks at the helm. The charismatic young man's high profile, resources, and deep commitment to the world of plants aligned perfectly with the visions of a royal family that delighted in the botanical realm.

Although goods from exotic lands had found their way to Europe since the days of Marco Polo, Joseph Banks's South Seas expedition with Cook marked the start of a new era. As more new life forms became available to study in Europe, they fed the hunger for even more, and an information revolution was born. Funding for scientists to accompany trade ships became normal; exploration developed into a regular component of the sea voyage. A livelihood as a natural history collector was possible for those willing to venture forth into the unknown. Banks's friend Margaret Bentinck would bring her influence, enthusiasm and resources to bear on this moment of progress in the field of natural history.

She was the only surviving child of Lord Harley and Henrietta Cavendish. Both Harleys and Cavendishes were deeply involved in the patronage and promotion of British science. Their daughter would singlehandedly elevate that tradition in her landmark contributions to the gathering, analysis and cataloguing of all manner of natural history objects. Her collection was astounding. On her death, its various components would take more than a month to be sold at auction.

Her childhood home was frequented by writers, scholars, politicians and philosophers. Her father was a renowned bibliophile; his spectacular private library founded the library of the British Museum. He was also a devoted gardener.

Her mother loved animals. In her youth Henrietta Holles had delighted in collecting unusual pets. The Governor of Barbados was a family friend, and from the tropics he sent the young Henrietta parakeets, land turtles, a Macaw, and a mysterious animal known only as a Jackawiney. The governor described the Jackawiney as "a diminutive lion not bigger than, and as tame as, a young rabbit."

Henrietta was also tremendously well read, growing up a favorite of the family librarian. But she was happiest in nature. Throughout her life she kept her own pack of harriers and was well-known for her prowess at riding and hunting.

Family connections on Margaret's husband's side also brought their influence to bear on her interests. Her father-in-law was the son of Willem Bentinck, whose gardens were famous. In 1686, John Evelyn, asked to recommend the finest gardens in Holland, sent his friends to visit Bentinck as well as to the grounds of two eminent Dutch lady collectors, Magdalena Poulle and Agnes Block. When William of Orange returned to England, he prevailed upon his good friend Bentinck to accompany him as Superintendent of Gardens.

Margaret's was a charmed youth. When she married the Duke of Portland, she became arguably the wealthiest woman in Europe. And William Bentinck was not only rich, he was reputed to be the handsomest man in England. Furthermore, they were compatible! Margaret described their marriage as "a union of love and friendship, but an exception to the general state." The Duke was her "sweet Will." He was neither ambitious nor political; family and patronage were the focus of their lives, and natural history was their particular pleasure. Theirs was a happy and generous life. They delighted in sharing their means by creating a serious salon for the natural history disciplines at their country home, Bulstrode. The menagerie and gardens Margaret created there would become very famous.

Bulstrode. Corbould 1794
Courtesy traditionalarchitecturegroup.org

Margaret began life as a duchess at nineteen. She remained close with all her childhood friends and much of their correspondence survives. The girls used code names in reporting news to one another, and often included word puzzles and riddles in their letters. They discussed books, theater and music. All had nicknames: Catherine Collingwood was Colly-flower or The Doctor, Mary Pendarves Delany was Pen, Elizabeth Wortley Montagu, Fidget. Fidget, who would become a founder of the Bluestocking

Society, called the Duchess 'Your Goodyship.'

These women were bright, funny, and well-educated. They were also well aware of the cardinal rule for females of the era: Reveal not a scintilla of interest in learning. Lady Mary Wortley Montagu, that paragon of propriety, put it clearly in advising her granddaughter that she "conceal whatever learning she attained with as much solicitude as she would hide crookedness or lameness."

And yet somehow, with no ado whatsoever, the Duchess of Portland set about creating a gathering place that became a renowned site of intellectual achievement over many years. The grounds of Bulstrode were the laboratory, her home the office, library and classroom.

Some say Margaret had the 'collecting gene.' Initially she acquired art, antiquities and porcelain. Over time, the natural world became her focus. Her shell collection was unparalleled. In creating her menageries and gardens, she began working with living things, and acquisition became not an end but the means to gaining knowledge of the field through the objects represented.

In the aviary visitors strolled among parrots, storks, peacocks, cranes, herons, bluebirds, nightingales, parakeets and five varieties of pheasant. There were bees, as well. Margaret and Mary Delany devoted a summer to creating a shell grotto from Margaret's shell collection. The Bulstrode menagerie boasted multiple varieties of sheep, buffalo, deer and hares. In recommending a visit to her cousin, Elizabeth Montagu says, "I believe the menagerie at Bulstrode is exceedingly well worth seeing, for the Duchess is as eager in collecting animals as if she foresaw another deluge, and was assembling every creature after its kind, to preserve the species."

Guests were also at liberty to wander through the American garden, botanic garden, shrubbery, flower garden, kitchen garden, ancient garden, and greenhouse. Her friend Mary Delany writes from Bulstrode: "The place is now in its full beauty and if any situation can bear a resemblance to paradise it is this. The variety of creatures (in perfect agreement) and vegetables are a constant scene of delight and amusement… a curious and enquiring mind cannot fail of being gratified."

Bulstrode came to be known as The Hive. It was constantly filled with activity, a place where philosophers, scientists, artists and royalty gathered, as "lively, intelligent conversation was always on offer." It stood apart from the other great houses of the time: It's distinction came not from fashion or attempts at spectacle or grandeur, but from the scholarly interests of the Duchess.

"Natural history is, at present, the favourite science over all Europe, and the progress which has been made in it will distinguish and characterize the 18th century in the annals of literature," said the Scottish naturalist Robert Ramsay. Much of this progress was made at Bulstrode, where collecting, cataloguing, and learning were the theme of daily life.

Margaret lost her beloved Will in 1761, and her commitment to botany intensified. Bulstrode was her refuge. She poured her time and resources into creating a personal Eden and gathering kindred spirits around her.

Plant taxonomy was still in flux. The Linnaean method was on the rise but had not completely supplanted the numerous systems that preceded it. The Duchess struck up a friendship with the French philosopher Jean-Jacques Rousseau, and it is interesting to see how the two approached the subject.

At the time, Rousseau was deeply in love. "I'm crazy about botany: It gets worse every day. I no longer have only hay in my head, I'm going to become a plant myself one of these mornings," he wrote. In 1776 he and Margaret botanized together on the moors of the Peak district. He adored Margaret and asked if she would be his botany teacher. Then he asked if he could add the title *Herbalist to the Duchess of Portland* to his name.

Rousseau was using a Linnaean book for plant taxonomy, but also Bauhin's botanical publication of 1623. The Duchess sent him a book she was using by Mary Somerset's friend James Petiver, as well as the classic work by John Ray, *Catalogus plantarum circa Cantabrigiam nascentium*, the standby of the 17th century.

They exchanged books and plants for some while after he regretfully took his leave for France. He did not refrain in expressing his fervor to Margaret in a dazzling string of metaphors: "I know one somewhat savage animal who would live with great pleasure in your menagerie, in awaiting the honor of being admitted one day as a mummy in your cabinet."

But their friendship ended abruptly. The Duchess sent Rousseau a lovely book about "exoticks," plants from the tropics. Rousseau was outraged: The idea of infringing on another culture's botanical world was in direct opposition to his reverence for the mythic Noble Savage, the pristine innocent, uncorrupted by civilization's touch. He deemed tropical botany "unnatural" for European pursuit. Rousseau and the Duchess were done. No matter—Mary Delany, a dear friend and widely considered the ultimate arbiter of taste and virtue, had not approved of the Frenchman anyway. She must have been piqued that it was in fact her brother who had introduced the two.

The flow of visitors at Bulstrode was constant. The acclaimed actors Mr. and Mrs. Garrick were friends. Philip Miller, the great botanical horticulturist, visited. Joseph Banks came often after the *Endeavour* expedition. He brought two important men, both of whom stayed.

John Lightfoot, the well-known parson-naturalist, became Margaret's chaplain and librarian. He served as curator to the Duchess's natural history collection, arriving at Bulstrode each Wednesday evening to lead prayers and remaining until Saturday to botanize, catalogue plants, and to engage family and guests in edifying conversation around new acquisitions. Of the Duchess, Lightfoot said: "Her goodness extends its influence to all who know her. Like the sun in the centre of the system all within her sphere are warmed by her genial virtues."

Parson-naturalists were a mainstay in the development of the natural sciences for many years in Britain. These men were well-trained and saw their engagement with studying the natural world as a continuum of their religious work. Mary Somerset's friend John Ray had been the pre-eminent example in his time. Mrs. Delaney notes in her diary during a visit to Bulstrode: "On Thu we shall return to a feast of reason (Lightfoot in residence)." Lightfoot would outlive the Duchess by several years, working alongside her to the end of her days. He was appointed a founding member of the Linnaean Society but died himself before the first meeting in 1788. His personal botanical collection was bought by King George III for Queen Charlotte.

Lightfoot was joined in cataloguing the Duchess's plants and shells by Daniel Solander, Banks' companion on the *Endeavour* voyage. Banks and Solander had come to Bulstode together in 1771 on their return to Europe, and gave seeds from the expedition to Margaret. She planted them in an area of her garden and mapped it as Botany Bay Field.

Solander divided his time between Bulstrode and the new British Museum, where he was organizing the massive collection of Sir Hans

Sloane. Solander had known Margaret before the journey through the Quaker plantsman Peter Collinson.

"Daniel Solander was a rather short, plump man of some thirteen stone, jovial, fond of company and much in demand in London society; he had a ready welcome for any Swedish visitors to England. Deeply affected by the marriage in 1764 of Linnaeus's eldest daughter, Elisabeth Christina, he became a confirmed bachelor. He was a popular conversationalist and 'a philosophical gossip,' notoriously forgetful and careless about his appearance, except for a weakness for elaborate waistcoats," said L.A. Gilbert.

Lady Elizabeth Montagu "Queen of the
Blues" Thomas Gainsborough before 1788
Courtesy Thomas-gainsborough.org

He was a favorite at Bulstrode. His cachet was surely enhanced when word got out that he had been involved in Swedish espionage as a young man. Apparently plantsmen, with their roving ways, were often approached to serve in a governmental capacity while on expeditions. Solander was also Linnaeus' star pupil and thus brought a deep understanding of the new classification system that was coming to dominate the world of science.

The two men became part of the Duchess' extended family, which also included several remarkable female members. One of the first was Elizabeth Montagu, whose friendship with Margaret began when Elizabeth was 12 and the Duchess 18 and continued throughout their lives. Bulstrode made a formidable impression on the young Elizabeth. In an era where women were constantly reminded to avoid knowledge and education at all cost, Elizabeth watched the Duchess miraculously circumvent the prevailing winds and create an exciting and powerful forum for intelligent conversation on serious topics. Furthermore, she found the Duchess' character consistently principled and unassuming.

Elizabeth put her experiences with the Duchess to good use. She became a founding member of the Bluestocking Society. The women of France had launched the salon tradition and Englishwomen followed, bringing along their own sensibilities. Elizabeth and several friends began organizing gatherings for informal discourse on philosophy, natural history and art. The Duchess attended, as did Mrs. Delany. The Bluestocking women succeeded in creating their own island of higher education, cleverly bypassing gender issues by the deceptively informal, social structure of the group. However, their commitment to knowledge was unwavering. As the group gathered momentum the focus became that of women in literature, and there were tremendous strides made in opportunities for women to publish.

Much of Elizabeth's correspondence remains intact. She was an excellent storyteller and very funny. Her nickname, Fidget, came from her comment that she did not know why a table needed 4 legs in order to stand still, when she could fidget on just two. She writes to Margaret: "No shepherdess on the plains of Arcadia had ever more rural amusements than my lady Duchess…you did not mention riding a milk white palfrey with captivated knights by your side but I suspect your grace only suppressed that part of your pastoral romance for fear I would not think it so humble as the spinning wheel. I expect to see you spinning so great a story as Penelope's web."

The spinning refers to Margaret's sterling reputation in handwork. She also wove, turned wood, and made lace. Feather fireplace screens were the height of fashion for some time, and the ones made by the Duchess were considered the finest.

Late in life Elizabeth reflected on her time at Bulstrode in a letter to Margaret: "I could easily give credit to all that could be said of the place and its queen, who, with her there have enjoyed the happiest days of my life… your Grace's conversation and example led me to a way of thinking which makes the happiness of all times and all seasons. You taught me neither to admire nor covet what was not really good."

Mary Delany, whom the famed orator Edmund Burke called "a woman of fashion for all ages" was arguably the Duchess's closest friend. Very bright and very well respected, she knew everyone and was tremendously talented. With her second husband she had created extensive gardens at Delville, their Irish estate where botanizing was a favorite pastime. Her reputation as a needlewoman was unparalleled. Lest we underestimate this skill, let us hear again from Lady Mary Wortley Montagu: "It is as scandalous for a woman not to know how to use a needle as for a man not to know how to use a sword."

Mary Delany's Burnet Rose
Courtesy British Museum

In her 70s, Mrs. Delany developed a completely new art form, her "paper mosaicks." These were astonishingly accurate botanical illustrations made of minute pieces of colored tissue paper cut and layered in unearthly precision. The works are not only beautiful, all backed on black paper, but also perfect botanically. More than one botanist commented that he preferred using Mrs. Delany's works for identifying plants above any other renderings. She created a catalogue of over 900 plants in only five years, beginning with the collections at Bulstrode. Depicting a Burnet rose she managed to create each stem—thorns and all—out of one piece of tissue.

After losing her husband, Mrs. Delany rusticated with the Duchess in Buckinghamshire each year for six months. It was at Bulstrode that the "Mosaicks" were born: One day, looking at a geranium in a vase sitting alongside a piece of tissue of a similar hue, Mrs. Delany picked up the tissue and began snipping and piecing. The Duchess entered the room and mistook Mrs. Delany's creation for an actual flower.

Bulstrode afforded Mrs. Delany access to hundreds of live botanical specimens. The King and Queen were frequent guests and tremendous fans. They arranged for Joseph Banks to supply her with additional plant samples from Kew. Searching for yet more plants to catalogue, she and Margaret would set out for Luton, the estate of her friend and neighbor the Earl of Bute, another serious plant collector, who in 1784 would publish his nine volume study of British plants. Only twelve copies of the work were printed and one was a gift to Margaret.

The Earl had played a large role in bringing botany to royal favor by sharing his interest and knowledge with Prince Frederick and Princess Augusta during his days as Prime Minister. His friendship with the dowager Princess continued after the death of the Prince and the ascent of George III. Word at Court was that the bounds of friendship had been exceeded, which resulted in a vertiginous fall from grace for the Earl. Fortunately, it allowed more time for gardening. He delighted in contributing to Mrs. Delany's studies.

Mrs. Delany recorded much of daily life at Bulstrode over the years in her diary. She joins Margaret and Dr. Lightfoot for botanical instruction. She disapproves of Rousseau. She gives detailed accounts of many visits to and from the Royal Family, as Buckingham Palace was a short carriage drive away. Of an upcoming tea with the King and Queen, she claims Margaret will bring her out to be examined with the other antiques. John Lightfoot chimes in when reporting to friends on the health of the household: "The Duchess goes on well, Mrs. Delany is immortal." One royal visit finds Mrs. Delany at her spinning wheel, and so the Queen is given instruction in the art. "She did tolerably well, for a Queen," said Mary.

Life at Bulstrode continued a happy affair. In 1745, Samuel Richardson wrote from Bulstrode to Dr. Young: "Virtue prudence peace industry ingenuity and amicableness dwell here." The Duchess possessed a sunny disposition and a tender heart. Her democratic nature was often remarked. Her gardener, Thomas Agnew, and her steward, Mr. Levers, regularly joined her and her guests in the drawing room to participate in collecting and organizing botanical samples and to share their own portfolios.

Nowadays, we take the existence of museums for granted. But in Margaret's time the concept was just taking shape. The fashion of collecting and assembling objects that were amazing and unique had begun during the Renaissance, initially as a personal and private endeavor. The product was known as a curiosity cabinet, or Wunderkammer (Cabinet of Wonders).

In assembling a cabinet, the ability to generate awe and wonder in the beholder was frankly every bit as valued as scientific pioneering. The Narwhal horn turned up in more than one display as the prized horn of the unicorn. A form of coral was exhibited as the hand of a mermaid. The line between the magical and the fantastically exotic was blurred for quite some time as science and classification caught up with discovery.

The intellectual gravitas that a cabinet bestowed on its owner was coveted. Of course, only those with the means to create and maintain a collection were able to engage in the activity. In the early modern times, the ways and laws of the wide world were being pondered by any and all, but for those with the ability to obtain the newest discoveries for study, the old adage applied: All opinions matter, but informed opinions matter more.

Whether the Duchess' assemblage at Bulstrode is best considered an early private museum or the ultimate curiosity cabinet, it was certainly at the vanguard. Nothing like it existed. How visitors experienced Margaret's collections is left to our imagination. The quantity of objects was enormous, containing representations of so many branches of art and science.

The Duchess of Northumberland commented that "in the Duchess' dressing room…there are 10000 curiosities." When a young Mary Hamilton came to Bulstrode, she wrote that the Duchess took her to her rooms on several occasions to view collections in drawers there. Elsewhere we hear that all the public rooms at Bulstrode were filled with displays. But as to the displays themselves, we have no information. Perhaps Bulstrode had many rooms filled with many, many shelves, cabinets and drawers!

Margaret continued adding to her plant specimens, actively cataloguing and classifying until her death. Although she was close with all her

Catalogue Cover, Duchess of Portland Auction 1786
Courtesy Biodiversity Heritage Library

children, none were much interested in her collections. She arranged to sell everything in order to generate capital for their estates.

Lightfoot assembled the auction catalogue, which totaled over 4000 lots comprised of jewels, paintings, silver, china, and her famous natural history collections. The event began on April 24, 1786, and continued for thirty-eight days.

The natural history portion of the sale lasted over a week. On the fourteenth day, it was recorded that her "dried plants, seeds, fungi, etc" were sold. This lot included "plant parcels from Africa, France, Tobago, Switzerland as well as England: A complete folio of English grasses; An outstanding collection of mosses catalogued in the Linnaean method: and many exotic seaweeds." The purchasers are unknown to us.

Lightfoot wrote to fellow naturalist Thomas Pennant: "This catalogue is not of the common stamp. The classical Names of the various subjects are religiously attended to. Dr. Solander's new Species are register'd & where figures existed, referred to. Much Pains have been taken in this Respect, in Hope of rendering the Catalogue worthy a Place in the Library of every Naturalist." Lightfoot's hopes were realized. Copies of the catalogue quickly became—and remain—tremendously collectible.

Two plants were named to commemorate the remarkable Margaret Bentinck. The first, a damask rose: Rosa Duchess of Portland; the second, Portlandia grandiflora, acknowledging Margaret's well-known insomnia: The sumptuous Portlandia comes to full fragrance at night, before dawn.

Margaret Bentinck created an oasis of learning that would have been a worthy accomplishment at any point in history; given the fashions and attitudes of her time, what she did at Bulstrode was nothing short of miraculous. The world was left a place of far greater possibility and knowledge as a result of her commitment and generosity.

Rosa Portlandia, H. C. Andrews. 1805
Courtesy Guttenberg Project

IV.

The
OPEN ROAD
by
ELEPHANT

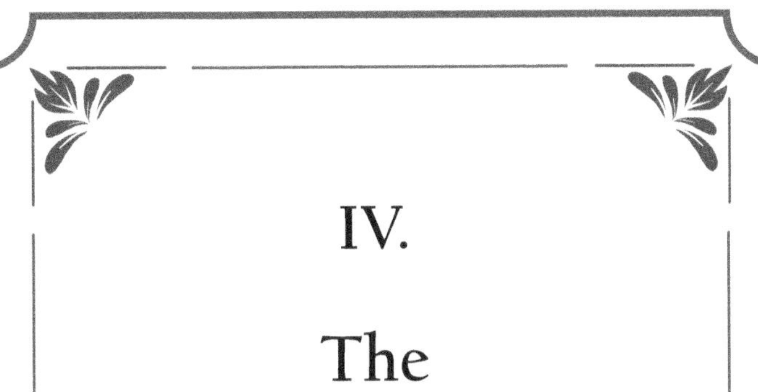

Lady Henrietta Clive
1758-1830

Henrietta Clive, Countess of Powis
by Sir Joshua Reynolds 1777
Courtesy National Trust

O N A STEAMY AUGUST AFTERNOON in 1798 Henrietta Clive first set foot in India. As the *HMS Dover* dropped anchor in the Bay of Bengal a flotilla of surf boats approached the frigate. There was no actual port at Madras, so Henrietta and her family were transferred to the smaller boats and rode the surf of the huge waves to shore. The Bay of Bengal breakers were notoriously fierce, but the distance from anchor to shore was only the span of three or four breakers and the passengers reached shore in a relatively dry state.

Lady Clive, her husband, and their two teenaged daughters had been en route to India for over six months. Their ship had sprung a leak and made port at the Cape of Good Hope for repairs. This impromptu stopover had been tremendously gratifying for Henrietta. She was interested in and knowledgeable about all facets of natural history, particularly plants. "I am sure nothing is like Africa…I set out tomorrow morning at daybreak and shall travel this country covered with the most beautiful flowers and heath," she writes to a friend. "We have found delightful plants and have scrambled til I can scarcely move," she reports a few days later. "Think of my extreme delight and ecstasy at finding many of the most beautiful plants which are poor creatures in our hothouses…all under our feet."

By happy coincidence, the superintendent of the Calcutta Botanical Garden had stopped over at the Cape as well, en route from India to England. Dr. Roxburgh shared seeds and plants with Henrietta, and a great deal of information about the natural history of India. He also arranged for her to work with his colleague Dr. Benjamin Heyne at the Madras Botanical Gardens on her arrival.

Before departing Africa she located an Indian botanist who agreed to collect for her. The famous botanists of earlier in the century were some twenty years gone. By the time Henrietta arrived, the plants which had met with success for naturalizing in Europe may well have all been identified, with the rest left to their native habitat. It was a disappointment to find no professional collectors on site, though judging from her remark about English hothouses, growing commercially available tropical plants in England was no guarantee of success.

Henrietta had been anticipating her great adventure in the exotic East for some time. Arriving in Madras to find a hot, provincial colonial outpost, she was sorely disappointed. "All is business and solitude," she finds. Years later Emma Roberts would still describe the experience of the European memsahib similarly: "Nearly unmitigated ennui is the lot of the majority of luckless (meaning European) women in India."

Henrietta, however, was not the majority, and she took steps forthwith. She engaged a Persian tutor for herself and the girls. "I am beginning Persian and hope in all due time to be able to read Hafiz and all the learned books. Then I shall be romantic and so extremely flowery in my discourse that I suppose I shall not be able to give a rational answer to a common question," she writes to her brother. In short order she had tackled a bit of that renowned Sufi poet in her diary: "In the banquet of life drink a cup or 2 and then depart. That is to say, entertain not a wish for perpetual enjoyment." Her teacher was so delighted with her progress he proposed Henrietta translate and publish a small volume, "as a pretty little epitome of eastern morality translated by an illustrious female oriental traveler." It was not to be; in short order, Lady Clive was simply too busy.

She started work on the grounds of the family's home, Garden House. A menagerie was begun. It included deer, baby bulls, antelope, several varieties of birds, and—briefly—a tiger. She set about working with Dr. Heyne, collecting and identifying the native flora to include in her garden. She prepared exports as well. Writing to Lady Douglas, she reports on having sent a bottle of seeds, some saved from the Cape, others from India. She located a second tutor for spoken Hindustani and created an impromptu classroom and "laboratory" for the girls. Daily they studied the plants, animals, butterflies, and rocks of India alongside music and drawing. They slowly acclimatized to the new culture, after some initial shocks. The girls attended their father's first public proclamation, and Henrietta reported they "could not be persuaded that the people dressed in long muslin dresses were not women, though some had long grey beards."

After a year in residence, fortune smiled on Henrietta in the unlikely form of Tipu Sultan, King of Mysore. The occasion of the journey to India was her husband Edward's posting as Governor of Madras, and the sultan's demise was a dramatic turn of events for the British in India. It also opened the way for Henrietta's great adventure.

The conquest of the fabulously wealthy kingdom of Mysore had eluded the British through three separate campaigns. In the particular, it had eluded Henrietta's father-in-law, Robert Clive, Clive of India. To this day, Clive of India holds the remarkable distinction of being viewed simultaneously as Britain's greatest and most reviled presence in India. He was brash and charismatic. His victory at Plassey is credited with establishing the political and military supremacy of the British East India Company, thereby laying the foundation for the era of the British Raj. The Company would become "a major imperial poser with a standing army and territorial possessions far larger than those of the country which gave it birth."

In this era Englishmen were returning from the East Indies in possession of outrageous and questionable fortunes. Clive himself came home to Britain the wealthiest self-made man in the country. On visiting Clive's home, Capability Brown saw a chest of gold on display. He wondered "how the conscience of the criminal [Clive] could suffer him to sleep with such an object so near his bedchamber." Horace Walpole weighed in as well, in a comment on rising prices in London: "I expect that a pint of milk will not be sold under a diamond, and then nobody can keep a cow but my Lord Clive."

Yet, as a soldier Clive had shown himself to be unarguably brilliant, his decisive victories at Arcot and Plassey securing British dominance in India. But Mysore was a thorn in his side.

Tipu Sultan was certainly a worthy opponent: sophisticated, learned, and a skilled tactician. On the battlefield, his reputation was one of immense savagery. After Tipu declared "'I would rather live one day as a tiger than a lifetime as a sheep," he became known as The Tiger of Mysore.

But he was very much a prince as well. He spoke five languages. His library was stocked with volumes on botany, astronomy, religion, history and medicine. After his death, the vast array of superb collections he had assembled came on the market and created a frenzy in Britain known as "Tipumania."

The empire, brought to its zenith by Tipu's father Haidar Ali, had been in existence since the 1300s. Both Tipu and Haidar were lovers of gardens. The two established India's first botanic garden, the Lal Bagh in Bangalore adjoining the King's palace.

Tipu Sultan Artist Unknown 1790-1800
Courtesy Freer Gallery of Art

'TIPU'S TIGER' 1793
A Mechanical Toy Created for Tipu Sultan
Courtesy The Victoria and Albert Musuem

During this period of the Carnatic Wars between the French and the British, Mysore allied with the French, a choice that would be its downfall. In 1788 Tipu sent an embassy to Paris to bolster military manpower. Despite the upheavals there, his men were the toast of the town. They returned laden with seeds, bulbs, gardeners, and clockmakers—but only a handful of soldiers.

Ten years on, he similarly sent a contingent to Mauritius. Again, it was a terrific botanical success—it took eighty men to deliver the plants, seeds and trees from the harbor. Politically, it sounded the death knell for the Kingdom of Mysore.

As Napoleon marched across Egypt, he was intent on clearing a path for conquest of the East Indies. Surely with a foothold in Mysore, overthrow of the British presence would come handily. Letters addressed to "The most magnificent Sultan, our Greatest friend, Tippoo Sahib" were flowing into the palace from Napoleon. Tipu's Mauritius embassy had returned with a mere 150 soldiers, but there were said to be thousands en route. Tipu donned a red cap and took to calling himself 'Citizen Tipu.'

One of Napoleon's letters fell into the hands of the British. The intelligence caused panic in London. Lord Clive had returned to England after two defeats against Mysore, so the moment fell to Lord Wellesley, serving as Governor General of Bengal. He seized the opportunity to request a dramatic boost in resources to put an end to the French in India once and for all. And so it was: The battle of Seringapatam in 1799 saw the Tiger of Mysore conquered and killed.

Tipu Sultan embodied the romance and the mystery of the unknown, exotic East. His wealth was nearly beyond measure, easily the largest Britain had ever attained in conquest. His connoisseurship was impeccable. And the fervor he unleashed was appalling: An officer attending his entombment reached out and cut off half of the dead man's mustache for a trophy.

And so a secret part of India fabled for its natural beauty, by and large unseen by any Europeans but soldiers, was opened. Henrietta saw her opportunity and seized it. She announced she was "determined to see as much as she could for a place so remarkable in the annals of this family." She would pay homage to King, Country and Clive by touring the smitten foe's kingdom. And coincidentally, she would experience India as she had intended, far from the doldrums of government camp.

When Henrietta Clive decided to botanize, it was an affair of state. The year was 1799, and she set out with twenty elephants, two camels, a hundred bullocks, and several hundred bearers. There were bearers for the bearers, their families, grooms, guards, a piano and a harp. Her daughters Henry and Charly, aged thirteen and fourteen, attended their mother, as did the Italian artist Anna Tonelli, who had accompanied the family to India. The journey would be many things: a great Oriental adventure, a groundbreaking natural history collecting expedition, a rolling embassy, even a classical Grand Tour. English persons took a Grand Tour of the European continent—why not one of India?

In no time Henrietta had assembled the aforementioned animals, people and objects, and off went the ladies. Over the months they would sleep in tents, in abandoned palaces and churches, and at royal Indian homes commandeered by British officials. Edward remained at his post in Madras.

"Charly" Clive 1799 by Anna Tonelli   Henry" Clive 1797 by Anna Tonelli
Courtesy Clive Museum Collection Powis Castle

Travel began each day no later than four in the morning to mitigate the heat. In her diaries, Charly remarked the jungle all around was "very tygerish." In one of their first encampments, an early morning cry of alarm awoke the party: In fact a bearer had been carried off by a tiger just before dawn. Alligators were regularly sighted. Huge scorpions made appearances.

The animals of India were much a part of their journey in other ways. The travelers were given gifts as they proceeded, many of them living: birds, antelope, a highly irritating monkey, and a gazelle. The gazelle was utterly tame and became Charly's beloved pet. One day at twilight the animal sadly ventured onto a second-floor patio and kept walking over the edge, with fatal results.

Henrietta was received by Tipu's numerous wives and children across the land, and a good deal of pomp greeted her procession generally. The Nautches of India are famous, and she reports unending troupes of delightful dancing girls. It amused her that although the Indians took tremendous pride in these formal dancing performances, the mere thought of a regular Indian woman—or worse, a European—dancing was a cause of utter dismay if not horror.

The Clive entourage totaled around seven hundred and fifty people; the expedition lasted the better part of a year and covered over a thousand miles. Young Charlotte was a quick study regarding the East Indies. Commenting on the size of the party in her diary, she said: "…it is not to be wondered at when all is considered, as traveling in India is not like traveling in Europe."

Maharajah Sarabhoji II, one of many rulers who received
Henrietta in India
Artist unknown, c. 1800
Courtesy Los Angeles County Museum of Art

The ladies visited numerous historic and holy sites. They were able to enter the Muslim temples, but none of the Hindu. Henrietta kept a journal, and Signora Tonelli captured visual impressions brilliantly with pen and watercolor. Charly must surely be the only pre-Victorian child whose papers—her diary of the journey—are housed in a major national archive, the British Library.

Meanwhile back at Garden House, Edward was tending the garden as well as the government. Himself a tireless gardener, runners kept him informed in detail of the natural world Henrietta was encountering.

Almost every letter from her remarked on seeds she was sending, or roses, or trees. The Signora painted redwoods and sandalwood, and Henrietta dug and sent each of these back to Edward.

"I will, if I can, bring many beans in my palanquin from Tanjore," wrote Henrietta. While in Tanjore she received the Rajah, his turban encrusted with pearls, astride a horse whose bridle was ornamented with diamonds and emeralds. She returned the visit of the Rajah and saw his "large royal tiger and hunting chita."

At Combaconum, Henrietta writes she "came through the most beautiful and rich country I ever saw by the side of the Cauvery." From Polachee: "I hope to have, while we are hereabouts, some specimens of the cardamom, pepper and cinnamon trees growing on the hills. I have sent some cuttings of a very curious sort of mistletoe with a beautiful flower. Pray have it grafted directly upon a tamarind tree…the moment you receive it." At Tranquebar: "I went to Dr. Rotthem to see his herbarium, which contains 4,000 specimens of plants. I have seen some plants of wood here from Sumatra, the most beautiful that can be found."

She requested her husband send out certain plants to her too, as many of her stopping places adjoined neglected gardens, which Henrietta insisted on sprucing up. When Edward informed Henrietta he was refurbishing Government House, her botanical importation program was substantially expanded: She had an entirely new piece of ground to house the botanical bounty of the journey.

Doulat Bagh

Doulat Bagh, Tipu's Bangalore summer palace, reminded her of France: "The garden not in great order but the situation is very pleasant and the whole being surrounded by walls and garden is more like Chantilly than any place I know." The fabulous Mughal gardens were influenced by their Persian roots, of course, as were the formal French gardens of the time.

In one letter, discussing the latest additions to her natural history trove, she writes to Edward that should there be such a thing as collectresses, she would like that very much. We join Henrietta in sincere regret there was not a formal role for women in that capacity. That she might have been a botanist in other times is remarked by several historians, as her knowledge and efforts were well beyond that of a hobbyist. We know she was the first European to collect *Caralluma umbellata*, and that she saw and identified *Gloriosa superba* and numerous aloes.

Caralluma Umbellata
Courtesy Gochwala Nursery India

One day she comments on having received "the best pineapple in India." It had been grown and sent by Edward! For her part she was sending plants not only home to the Governor but on by ship to England as well, though the correspondence lag was so slow from Europe to the

Indies that she was often left hanging for news of safe arrival. She regularly inquired of Edward 'from the track' if certain plants had arrived for her from England.

At Government House, Edward succeeded in grafting a mango tree and sent it off to Kew Gardens. "If they should succeed in thriving in Britain, I might be tempted to construct a (hot) House for that purpose should you have no apprehension of being rated (i.e., *known as*) my lady Mango," he tells Henrietta.

Arriving at Bangalore, the ladies found the conquering hero Colonel Wellesley, who had made his residence in Tipu's zenana, the harem compound adjoining the palace. He insisted Henrietta's party join him there, despite her plans to stay several miles away at the Lal Bagh, where the tombs of Tipu and his father are located. It was a serendipitous change of plans. In the palace, Henrietta was introduced to a wondrous new invention, the Sultan's personal creation: a shower. Utterly enraptured, she sent word one must be constructed at Government House forthwith.

Henrietta's journey made a circuit of what was known as 'The Great Horn.' The farther the group ventured from Madras, the more delightful she found the scenery. Welcome relief from the heat accompanied the high country, and all felt a lift in spirits. Henrietta was keeping a close watch on her daughters, assessing if the family was strong enough to withstand the tropics for the length of Edward's term.

By the time the ladies arrived back in Madras, her decision was made. She felt it was best for her, the girls and Signora Tonelli to depart directly. With her went not only her collected natural history treasures and much of the menagerie, but the Clive family's own Tipu memorabilia. His fabulous tent came with Henrietta, and she continued his custom of erecting it in the garden for parties. There were gold ornaments from Tipu's throne. Perhaps the most remarkable of Tipu's posessions the Clives acquired was as far from an Eastern relic as could be imagined: a set of Sèvres China teacups given by Louis XVI to Tipu in happier times. Astonishingly, these survived in perfect condition their trip from France to Mysore, and then from Mysore to Liverpool, and can be viewed today.

Edward returned from India the following year, having fulfilled his term, and is kindly remembered for demanding increased pay for Indian soldiers.

Powis Castle
Courtesy The National Trust

He would outlive Henrietta by nine years, gardening to the end of his days. "Remarkable for his physical vigour he might be seen, when about eighty, digging in his garden at six o'clock in the morning in his shirt sleeves."

In her early days at Madras Henrietta wrote "I cannot sit and be idle." Nor did she! While preparing for her departure from India she assembled an herbarium which contained a complete sampling of the plants of the Carnatic region. Working with Dr. Heyne's assistant, she catalogued all her findings from her tour as well: animal, vegetable and mineral.

The expedition she created and undertook was utterly unique from every point of view. She and her daughters saw festivals and temples. They received and were received by holy men, fakirs, rajahs, sultans and their families. They collected plants and minerals as well as cultural artifacts. They witnessed tiger hunts and rode elephants.

Two hundred years have passed since Henrietta's journey. Through her letters, diaries, and collections, we see a world no European woman had experienced, and share the remarkable Oriental adventure she had her heart set on.

Powis Castle, which passed into the Clive family when Edward married Henrietta, houses to this day one of the foremost collections of Indian artifacts, though finally there are woefully long overdue plans for reparation.

In 1828, *Clivia nobilis* was recorded and named in honor of Henrietta, the noble family of Clive, and of Henrietta's daughter, Charly, the Duchess of Northumberland, in whose garden it first bloomed in England.

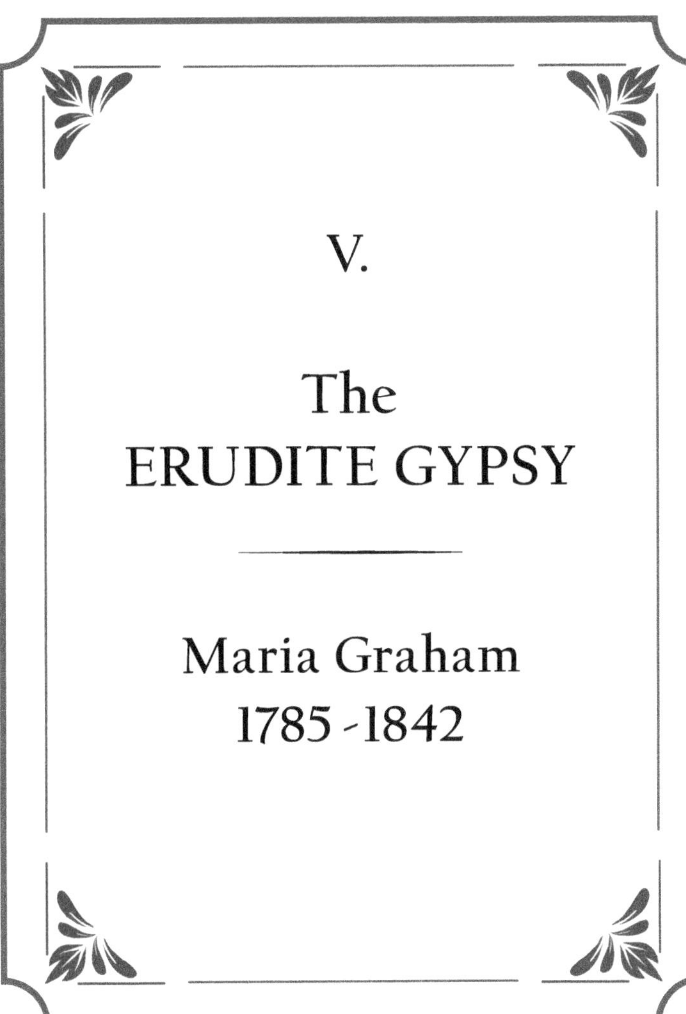

V.

The
ERUDITE GYPSY

Maria Graham
1785 - 1842

Maria Graham by Augustus Wall Calcott c.1830
Courtesy Government Art Collection

"**I** LIKE THIS WILD LIFE WE ARE LIVING, half in the open air; everything is an incident; and as we never know who is to come, or what is to happen next, we have the constant stimulus of curiosity to bear us to the end of every day."

Maria Graham wrote these lines in 1822, from a beachfront lean-to near Valparaiso, Chile. The famous 8.5 magnitude earthquake had just occurred, and her household had decamped to open ground. Her home had inconveniently been declared a holy site, as it had been untouched. "The priests resolved to make a miracle of it; and accordingly… Nuestra Senora del Pilar was found in her satin gown standing close to my stove, and received numerous offerings for having protected the premises."

She likened the sound of the quake to what she had heard while standing on the cone of Vesuvius during an eruption in 1818. In Chile, she witnessed the tectonic coastal uplift which occurred as a result of the earthquake, an event which had never been recorded. She did so.

Her account was published in the Royal Geographic Society Journal. The president of the Society raised a great hue and cry, contesting her findings. Both her husband and her brother offered to duel the truculent Mr. Greenough on her behalf, but Maria chose instead to engage in a very pointed and public discourse on the matter. She was proven to be completely accurate in her observations and conclusions; it seemed the only problem with her report was her gender. Charles Darwin would exonerate her doubly, confirming her findings while on board the Beagle the following year.

At the time of the exchange with Mr. Greenough, Maria was a published author, and a very successful one. She was 27 when *Journal of a Voyage to India* went to press, the first of 13 books she wrote, illustrated, and published. Fantastically intelligent, talented, educated and prickly, Maria would continue to chafe at the constraints of society all her life. She traveled to Italy, Portugal, Tenerife, Madeira, India, Ceylon, Brazil and Chile before the age of 30. These trips were the foundations for her first publications, diaries of her travels.

Maria knew her history and literature, and her botanical knowledge was very strong. Her iconoclasm and keen mind combined to create a real magic in bringing foreign lands to life through her words. In South America, she recorded in real time the dramatic battles for independence in both Chile and Brazil. Very few Europeans, and no other European women, saw fit to provide a firsthand account of the historic events taking place in the two countries.

Maria's unfettered Scottish country childhood had ended when she was eight years old. Her mother was unwell; Maria was taken away and the two would not meet again. She was deposited in the household of an uncle in Richmond. He was Sir David Dundas, doctor to George IV. His household was formal: The ladies were to take interest exclusively in clothing and all things French, no more. There Maria came to know the Prince of Wales, Lady Bessbrough, and their circle. Although her Richmond family was kind, it was an unhappy and uncomfortable situation. Everyone knew Maria's father had no fortune and thus there were no prospects for the girl in Society.

Boarding school was her next home, and things started out well enough. She took to the two Misses Bright, the sister headmistresses, and they to her. At the age of 10, she was given charge of geography lessons for the younger children, and a border in the garden for her own.

The natural world was her delight. "There was no end to the treasure of plants this marshy plain furnished, and with Withering tucked under my arm…by the side of my governess…I have often thought myself the happiest creature in the world, while she shewed me how to compare the plants with the description in the book." But Maria's precociousness was accompanied by a terrifically violent temper. After a series of vicious episodes, the teachers isolated her from the other children and from her studies for some months.

The room where she was quarantined held shelves filled with the headmistress's favorite books. Maria spent the solitary days reading Pope's translations of Homer's *Iliad*, Dryden's translations of Virgil, and much of Shakespeare. Her teachers' soft-heartedness made itself known when Maria realized the books were disappearing and being replaced as she worked her way through them. By the age of 11, Maria Graham was more well-read than most of her contemporaries would be in their lifetime.

When Maria was readmitted to her studies she was taken to see the formidable botanical collection of the Bishop of Durham, to Walpole's gardens at Strawberry Hill, and to the Oxford Physic Garden, where she reconnected with the delight of gardens, plants and plant classification.

Edinburgh was her next home, with another uncle. This uncle was more involved in the intellectual circles of Society. These were the first years of the prestigious Edinburgh Review, and Maria spent time with many of the men involved. Their areas of expertise ranged from literature and philosophy to mathematics. At balls, "I was always a bad dancer… and very much preferred sitting by and talking with the professors, who were obliging enough to put up with… a real desire to learn, and a true respect for philosophy."

Despite the kindness extended to Maria by the older men, societal prejudice existed too in Edinburgh. Maria's forthright, stormy nature and intellectual strength gained her a mixed reception. She was also diagnosed with tuberculosis at that time. Once again placed in isolation, she adored the chance to do nothing but read and draw for a prolonged period. She breezed through Gibbons' *Decline and Fall of the Roman Empire* and Dante's *Inferno*.

1808 found her recuperated and bound for Bombay with her father, sister, and brother. Her father, his naval fighting days behind him, had been appointed Commissioner of the Navy in India.

She recorded everything. They put in at Madeira, and she ate her first banana: "Agreeable, but wants the lightness and spirit one wishes for a fruit." She visited a garden built by a Mr. Murdoch, who had collected plants from the four corners of the Earth, and saw "orange, lime, citron, lemon myrtle, dragon gum palm, Sago, mimosa, laurel, coffee tulip tree, Mellaleuca Camellia j., jasmine, as well as native purple lotus, geranium, heathers."

Tenerife was the next port of call, and home to the Dragon Tree (*Dracaena draco*), sacred tree of the Guache. Maria went ashore to visit and draw the tree, reputed to be over 2000 years old and "now a noble ruin." Those drawings now reside alongside her botanical recordings in the British Museum.

Dragon Tree and Peak Of Tenerife by Maria Graham c.1824
Courtesy U.S. Library of Congress Rare Books and Special Collections Division

Putting in at Capetown, Maria found there were no plant collectors or collections, but a gardening Navy Captain made her a gift of amaryllis, belladonna, hyacinth, pelargoniums and seeds to plant in Bombay.

On board, romance blossomed between Maria and one of the Scottish officers, and by the time the ship docked in Bombay, she was engaged to Thomas Graham. Awaiting the nuptials, Maria immersed herself fully in India. She visited bazaars, temples and native households. She captured the architecture, religious ceremonies, festivals, customs and dress of the land in her diary. She described and sketched the geography and particularly the vegetation in detail.

Of the grounds of her Bombay house she says: "Our garden is delightful…we are always sheltered from the sun by the fan-like heads the palmyras, whose tall columnar stems… serve to support an innumerable variety of parasite and creeping plants, which decorate their rough bark with the gayest hues, vying with the beautiful shrubs which flourish beneath, and affording shelter to birds more beautiful than themselves." Beds are filled with fruits and flowers: "jasmine, roses, tuberoses, plumbagos, ixoras, mulberry and oleander, moon-flower and mogree."

She was free with her judgments as well. Indeed, this would be a hall-mark of her journals. Of the "Hindoos" she says: "I every day find some traces of the manners and simplicity of the antique ages; but the arts and the virtues that adorned them are sunk in the years of slavery under which the devoted Hindoos have bent."

She had no better to say for her own European contingent: "The parties in Bombay are the most dull and uncomfortable meetings one can imagine."

Her struggles with ill health continued in India. When bedridden, she doubled down on her Persian studies, her tutor a well-known scholar who visited daily. An ocean voyage was prescribed, and Maria and Thomas headed to Ceylon. "I am so delighted with the place…that if I could choose my place of residence for the rest of the time of my absence from England, it should be Columbo." She rides an elephant and has a chance to see the giant baboons in the trees. She visits the cinnamon gardens, finds cashews and datura, and provides detailed descriptions of native plants she cannot identify.

The Ceylonese guest houses charmed her: "The rest-house was decorated with white and coloured calico tied up in roses, and coco-nut leaves split so as to form fringes and festoons; the pillars of the viranda were covered with palm leaves tied up in bunches, and a gateway at a little distance was dressed in the manner of a triumphal arch, with leaves and many-coloured flowers."

Returning to the mainland, visiting Madras, she pronounced the European community there only marginally more elegant than that of Bombay, but was delighted with the famed Madras jugglers and sword swallowers. She visited the hospital and the orphanage, and in an abandoned private botanical garden she found nopal and *Sagus rumphii* flourishing.

At Calcutta she stayed at Government House. At long last Maria declares that in Calcutta, English society afforded "a greater portion of intellectual refinement." Of the nearby port of Barrackpore, she remarked: "There is something in the scenery of this place that reminds me of the beauty of the banks of the Thames."

Maria disregarded the tradition of averting one's eyes from foreign customs perceived as savage, cruel or gruesome, to say nothing of unlady-like. Suttee, the rite wherein the Hindu widow is expected to join the burial pyre of her husband, is described in some detail in her diary. And although she loved Barrakpore, she devoted a full page to describing an encounter with a dead body being torn apart by jackals. She also described the custom of taking the infirm to the banks of the river and filling their noses and mouths with mud, that they might expire more quickly.

In Calcutta she also had William Roxburgh's wonderful Calcutta Botanic Garden. Roxburgh was Scottish and contemporaneous with the professors who had befriended her in Edinburgh, so likely Maria was quickly at her ease with him. She spent time with the Roxburgh family and showed again the breadth of her botanical knowledge as she recorded in her diary not only the plants she saw but also their uses in folk medicines.

"After having visited the garden, Dr Roxburgh obligingly allowed me to see his native artists at work, drawing some of the most rare of his botanical treasures; they are the most beautiful and correct delineations of flowers I ever saw. Indeed, the Hindoos excel in all minute works of this kind," she says.

With her husband recalled to England, Maria set sail to join him there. Stopping in at the Cape, she included discussions of *Protea argentea* and *Protea Mellifera* in her writings, with their many uses. At St. Helena, too, she reported on the trees she found, and the large variety of fruits.

Once home, her India journal and illustrations were published to great success. Her portrait of the mysterious East was compelling, scholarly, and conversational all at once. Her frame of reference was erudite, and it earned her the respect of readers of both sexes. Her voice was a singular mixture of cultural observation and commentary, of drama and romance—with just the right dollop of Gothic flair.

Of course she would always have her detractors. In 1815, Lady Anne Romilly wrote to a friend regarding Maria: "She is writing again, I'm sorry to say, on Heathen Mythology; one cannot read it." This was doubtless a reference to Maria's second publication, *Letters on India*, a historical study of Indian culture.

Finding herself at home in the Scottish countryside, her husband on leave with peacetime half-pay, Maria was restless for her next adventure. Her publisher, John Murray, arranged for her to be seated next to a

Navy Admiral at a dinner party, in hopes of advancing a commission for her husband. Instead a political row ensued between the dignitary and Mrs. Graham. Yet, a few weeks later the man reported to Murray that he admired a spirited woman and offered Col. Graham a commission.

The Grahams, now Captain and Mrs., departed for South America aboard the *HMS Doris*. The ship was charged with scouting the coastline, protecting British trade interests and staying abreast of rebel uprisings. En route Maria kept records of her botanical explorations at Funchal, and again at Tenerife.

Her first South American diary began as soon as the ship set sail. Aboard the *Doris*, she organized a school for the younger sailors, and marked the famous Father Neptune ceremony on crossing the equator. Shipboard the doors of her cabin were always open and well used, as it was both floating classroom and infirmary.

Arriving in Brazil in 1822, the British contingent finds Pernambuco is under siege by rebel forces. The *Doris* stays at anchor, though Maria goes ashore and botanizes on numerous occasions. She gives a charming account of a picnic with the midshipmen and officers, noting plants, butterflies and birds: "The very reptiles are beautiful here."

As matters stabilize in Pernambuco, the *Doris* sets sail for Bahia, where things are more peaceful. Maria says, "We rode out before breakfast through landscape so fine, that I wished for a poet or a painter at every step." She sees gamelan trees and several varieties of tillandsia.

Again we receive her commentary on the people she meets. Initially she finds Portuguese women are "almost indecently slovenly," but reconsiders quickly. Attending a party at the home of the consul, she "had great difficulty in recognizing the slatterns of the other morning." In Brazil, one received one's callers a bit later in the day than in England, and in fact the ladies had simply not been dressed for receiving.

She has the chance to botanize often and extensively and describes the land with great heart: "I rode out along the banks of the lake, decidedly the most beautiful scenery in this beautiful country; and then through wild groves, where all the splendours of Brazilian animal and vegetable life were displayed. The gaudy plumage of the birds, the brilliant hues of the insects, the size, and shape, and colour, and fragrance, of the flowers and shrubs, seen mostly for the first time, enchanted us."

Corcovado From Botofago by Maria Graham c.1824
Courtesy Instituto Moreira Salles Rio de Jaineiro

Skirmishes between the Portuguese and the guerillas abate, and the Doris makes way for Rio de Janeiro. "Nothing that I have seen is comparable in beauty to this bay," she says of Corcovado. The Grahams find accommodations on shore, and Maria spends her days riding and exploring the flora and visiting the Botanic Garden. The Rio garden is organized exclusively for experimenting on imported plants for commercial use, with no indigenous plants represented.

As to the British of Rio, Maria opines, "they are very like all one sees at home; and the ladies, very good persons doubtless, would require Miss Austin's pen to make them interesting." Is she referring to Jane Austen? Maria's spelling is consistently inconsistent, in keeping with the style of the times; they did share the same publisher.

She predictably botanizes while visiting friends in the countryside. "Every turn in our ride brought a new and varied landscape into view: beneath, the sugar-cane in luxuriant growth; above, the ripening orange. And the palm; around and scattered through the plain enlivened by the windings of the Guazidiba, the lime, the guava, and a thousand odorous and splendid shrubs beautified the path—But all is new here."

Maria hears the slaves singing from their adjacent settlement after supper one evening and promptly sets out for their village to join the merriment, describing their music and instruments in great detail. From her description of the outing, she was welcomed.

The Doris weighs anchor again, bound for Chile. Captain Graham takes ill and before the ship makes port he has died. Maria goes ashore in Valparaiso to gather her wits. Rejecting offers of transport back to Europe, she takes a small house for herself and her ailing sailor cousin, not in the European quarter but on the edge of town.

With Captain Graham's death Maria stopped the diary she had been writing and began a new volume, *Journal of a Residence in Chile.* Later she added an introduction to the work: "There is not shipwreck in every canto indeed," she says, "but I have earthquake and civil war, calamities enough I assure you to last a lifetime."

Her first entries are of tentative outings, walks exploring the land around her cottage, with detailed notes on the flowers and shrubs. Descriptions of the geography, the town and its buildings follow. She makes the acquaintance of her neighbor and is introduced to the national ritual of mate drinking. Soon she is giving splendid accounts of the local clothing, hair, fashions, food, and shops.

She devotes a great deal of time to botanical rambles during this period and records them in detail. "The shrubs are beautiful, and mixed here and there with the Chilian aloe (Pourretia coarctata), and the great torch thistle, which rises to an extraordinary height … I remarked varieties of our common garden herbs, caraway, fennel, sage, thyme, mint, rue, wild carrot, and several sorts of sorrel. But it is not yet the season of flowers: Here and there only, a solitary fuschia or andromaeda was to be found." She encounters a grove of *Palma tehera.* Having never seen a palm like it, she describes it at great length.

View of Quintero Bay, Chile by Maria Graham
Courtesy archive.org

Maria has been in residence for five weeks when a ship arrives in port to tremendous fanfare. It bears Thomas Cochrane, the great British naval hero dubbed 'The Sea Wolf' by Napoleon.

Maria's friendship with Cochrane develops quickly. The great man is in Chile to lead the country's battle for independence from Portugal, which he accomplishes handily. Maria writes a long exposition in her journal of the turbulent history and politics of Chile. She places Lord Cochrane at the center of her story, and it seems likely that he is the primary source for her political views. She lionizes him: "If I ever met with genius I should say it was pre-eminent in Lord Cochrane."

And she continues exploring, mounting an expedition to Santiago accompanied by a British midshipman and three pack mules. Of her chosen route she says: "I wonder that I have never heard the beauty of this road praised… In short, it might have been Italy, but that it wanted the tower and the temple to show that man inhabited it: But here all is too new; and one half expects to hear a panther roar from the hill."

She stays with friends of friends in the country outside Santiago for some time: "I may repeat, a thousand times over, 'tis the loveliest day I have seen; for, in the fresh untouched scenes of nature, each succeeding one is lovelier than the last. The star-like flower beneath my feet, the magnificent purple shrub that drapes over the cliff…all, all were beautiful. The scenery reminded me of that around the Lago Maggiore."

Thomas Cochrane, The Sea Wolf by James Ramsay c.1830
Courtesy Society for Hellenism and Philhellenism

Maria had the wisdom and curiosity to not only record the plants she saw, but to seek out information from the local populace on their usages in the community. This was truly invaluable data, gathered for the first time by a European.

On her return to Valparaiso, she is invited to accompany Lord Cochrane on an outing to his estate at Quintero Bay. Their small ship is the very first steam vessel to navigate the Pacific; Maria, a seasoned sailor, is amazed and delighted by the novelty.

Returning to her home from the village one day, she finds a visitor of renown at her home: General San Martin, the "Protector of Peru." It was San Martin who engaged Lord Cochrane to assist in consolidating the liberation of Chile. The General had then been rejected to assist in Peru by Simon Bolivar. Maria was privy to the details of Lord Cochrane's relations with the General, which had become quite strained. She has no inkling if her visitor is under house arrest or an honored guest in the country but makes room for his entourage of 16. The General holds forth on politics, religion, and philosophy well into the night. She is unimpressed with his intellect but concedes his charm in commenting that his reputation for being a delight in the ballroom is likely well deserved. "There is no one I'd rather spend 30 minutes with" is her cool appraisal. Soon San Martin's status is clarified: He has taken up residence at the palace.

The drama of formation of the new government of Chile continues, as does Maria's love of South America: "I cannot conceive a finer climate than that of Chile, or one more delightful to inhabit; and now I am accustomed to the trembling of the earth, even that seems a less evil than I could have imagined."

Several weeks after San Martin's visit finds Maria passing a quiet evening with friends, when the earth trembles rather more dramatically. The famous earthquake of 1812 occurs. The party and her household flee to open ground. The devastation is dramatic and the aftershocks continue for weeks. Returning to investigate the state of her house as the crisis abates, she finds it quite sound. But, news of its miraculous survival had spread, and it has been rented to a higher bidder in her brief absence.

As she packs her belongings, an unexpected offer arrives: Lord Cochrane suggests she join his party on their voyage to Brazil. Cochrane's services have been retained for this next battle for independence.

Maria accepts. As their departure approaches she walks out one morning with Lord Cochrane. "I will in all probability never again see the place, where, in spite of much suffering, I have also enjoyed much pleasure. We gathered many seeds and roots, which I hope to see springing up in my own land, to remind me of this, where I have met with a kindness and a hospitality never to be forgotten." Maria later added a note to this passage: "While this sheet was in the press one of the bulbous roots, called in Chile Mancaya, flowered in the garden of Messrs. Lee and Kennedy at Hammersmith. It is now called the *Cyrtanthia Cochranea.*"

Once in Rio de Jainero, Maria botanizes and gathers fruit daily. The officers "are enraptured with the wild Beauty of the scenery and have brought many splendid flowers and shrubs—the giant fuchsia andromedas and myrtles; but above all, a lovely monopetalous flowering shrub: The leaves are thick set, shiny green; the flower and berry of the riches purple. I never saw anything like it." We, too, are left with the mystery.

News arrives that Lady Cochrane is also making her way to Rio, having been absent in Europe for a year. Maria predictably finds herself snubbed by local British society, as she has been regularly at Lord Cochrane's side. She soldiers on. Lady Cochrane arrives; at a ball with only three other Englishwomen, including Lady Cochrane, a gentleman remarks that the four hardly conversed together. Maria addresses his comment headlong in her diary: "This was perfectly true: I like when I am in foreign society to talk to foreigners; and think it neither wise nor civil to form coteries with those of one's own nation in such cases."

Although much in character, it is possible the lady protested too much. A hallmark of Maria's character was an air of disdain, often evoking a coolness towards her in the European communities she encountered abroad as well as in England. Despite her experience in Rio, she was unwavering in her loyalty and support of Lord Cochrane throughout the years, although the two would not meet again.

On the other hand, Maria's status as an educated British lady, newly widowed, stood her in good stead with the Portuguese nobility. The Austrian Empress of Brazil, Leopoldine, became a valued ally as well. The two women shared a passion for natural history, and their friendship would last until the Empress's death, long after Maria's time in Brazil.

And so, Maria stays on. She is regularly confronted with the presence of slavery, which had already been outlawed in Britain. She encounters the slave market and approaches a group of children in a house used as a slave depot. "I went and stood near them, and though certainly more disposed to weep, I forced myself to smile to them, and look cheerfully, and kissed my hand to them." Despite prolific landscape sketches, she cannot bring herself to put pencil to paper at the slave market and uses the drawing of a colleague in her manuscript.

She witnesses a slave burial, which consisted of dragging the corpse to the shore, that the surf might attend to disposing of the body. Returning from the beach she encounters a Catholic priest leading a burial procession with all the customary pomp. The contrast causes her to remark: "But man, vain man, plays such fantastic tricks before high heaven as make the angels weep."

She organizes a brief expedition to Santa Cruz, fourteen leagues from Rio, accompanied by the brother of a friend, a Mr. Dampier. Botanizing

Princess Leopoldine by Josef Kreutzinger 1815
Courtesy Shonbrunn Palace Collection

on the way, she says: "Every time I pass through a grove in Brazil, I see new flowers and plants, and a richness of vegetation that seems inexhaustible. Today I saw passion flowers of colours I never observed before; green, pink, scarlet, and blue; wild pine apples, of beautiful crimson and purple; wild tea, even more beautiful than the elegant Chinese shrub; marsh palms, and innumerable aquatic plants new to me."

Returning to the capital, Maria receives word that independence has been gained, and the young Portuguese prince Don Pedro will stay. He has ignored orders to return home, changed allegiance, and accepted the title of Emperor of Brazil. Maria turns to Empress Leopoldine and puts herself forward as governess for the royal princess. She is offered the post and wastes no time in setting sail for England to gather supplies.

But, she is dismissed by the Emperor immediately on her return, due to political complications. As in Chile, she stays on against all odds with no prospects. During her earlier stay she had spent a great deal of time exploring the plants and land at Laranjeiras, and friends there offer her a cottage.

Endlessly resourceful, Maria begins a correspondence with William Hooker. The famed botanist is serving as the first formal director at Kew, and he entreats her to collect for him in Brazil. She replies: "I am very very fond of plants & scruple neither muddy feet nor torn clothes for their sake."

As 1825 begins, she sends this note to Hooker: "The other day a thunderstorm floated my parlour—& for three days my mountain torrent was so high I had no communication with the rest of the world. However I will make you envious: In the first place my cottage is known by its tree the Crataeva or garlic pear, the largest & finest I ever saw—it has not blossomed since I came though. Then the hedge, besides coffee, cotton, Bombax pentandrum, castor oil nut & limes, is very gay with Bauhinia, the large white."

Maria sent back over twenty-two varieties of Brazilian fern to Hooker. She found them all growing in the area between her cottage and the top of Corcovado. The Kew archives hold 100 illustrations she made of the plants she sent, with notes and descriptions. Like her fellow tropical collectors in the pre-Wardian era, she struggled with the challenge of the ravages of insects, and with the difficulty of drying plants in the humid climate, particularly the fleshy plants. Thus she chose to capture many of the plants through drawings and produced a botanical compendium of the Brazilian flora.

In 1827, Hooker would name an entire genus, Grahamae, after her, as well as a particular plant, *Escallonia calcottiae*. In 1841, he published his *Botanical Miscellany* and included many of Maria's botanical illustrations of Brazil. Her observations were regularly referred to in botanical journals of the time by scientific colleagues. David Douglas complimented "her talented pencil." "A highly accomplished English lady," said Carl Von Martius, who relied heavily on her findings in his *Flora Brasiliensis*. "An ingenious and sensible authoress," said John Sims, publisher of the *Curtis Botanical Magazine.*

Letter from Maria Graham to William Hooker, April 1824
Courtesy British Museum

In 1825 Maria headed for home, where her writing career continued to flourish. Her Chilean and Brazilian journals were both well-received and would stand the test of time. They have remained in continuous publication to this day. Alongside the record of her experiences and impressions, each journal devotes over 100 pages presenting the political backdrop for the two revolutions she witnessed.

Maria remarried and settled in London at Kensington Gravel Pits. Her second husband was a well-known artist, Augustus Wall Calcott. The two travelled together throughout Europe, this time the focus of her travels being art. Maria had already published a biography of Poussin and penned several more works on art and art history. The Calcotts' home was a popular gathering place for artists of the time.

Maria's health was failing by the time she reached her fifties, but her creative output did not slow. *Little Arthur's History of England,* her wildly popular children's book, sold over 1 million copies. *The Little Bracken-burners* and *Mary's Four Walks*, a two-part volume for children, were again filled with her love of the natural world. *Mary's Four Walks* is a charming tale of a little girl's outings in the country, each chapter closing with lists of the plants she encountered, including their botanical names and their uses.

Maria, now Lady Calcott, spent her final days in the compound that had been in the Calcott family for generations. The Calcotts were a large and close-knit family, and there was a constant to and fro of relations in the compound. Her many nieces were particularly close with Maria and visited frequently. Perhaps her prickly nature was softening.

Her last book, *A Scripture Herbal*, is surely her most poignant work. In it, she discussed each plant mentioned in the Bible, with stories about its origin, history, and uses. Each place in the Bible where the plant is mentioned was noted, and each included a botanical drawing, mostly by Maria. Completely bedridden, her claim that this last work was indeed "a labour but a labour of love" was literally true.

As a young woman, Maria said: "There is no class of life in which … knowledge and taste can be a disadvantage to a woman. They render her independent of what are termed the pleasures of the world; they can cheer the dullest home." And thus did she live.

The depth and breadth of knowledge Maria Graham possessed was exceptional for any individual at any point in history. She undertook adventures far beyond the reach of most men of her time, much less women. She redefined the possibilities for women with professional aspirations. Her contributions to botany were prodigious and groundbreaking. She is remembered for them, for her writings, and for her art.

Maria seized every opportunity to create a life that was tailored to her unique strengths and appetites. Society struggled with Maria, and she with it. Unwilling to compromise, she set about pursuing a life of freedom and adventure. And in so doing, she amassed a remarkable body of work. She did so despite ill health throughout her life and died at age 57. To this day, her journals are read and referred to in scholarly works internationally. Surely the young girl nicknamed "Metaphysics in Muslin" by her Edinburgh professor friends would have taken enormous pleasure and pride in her formidable legacy.

Escallonia Calcottiae
Courtesy Royal Botanical Gardens of Edinburgh

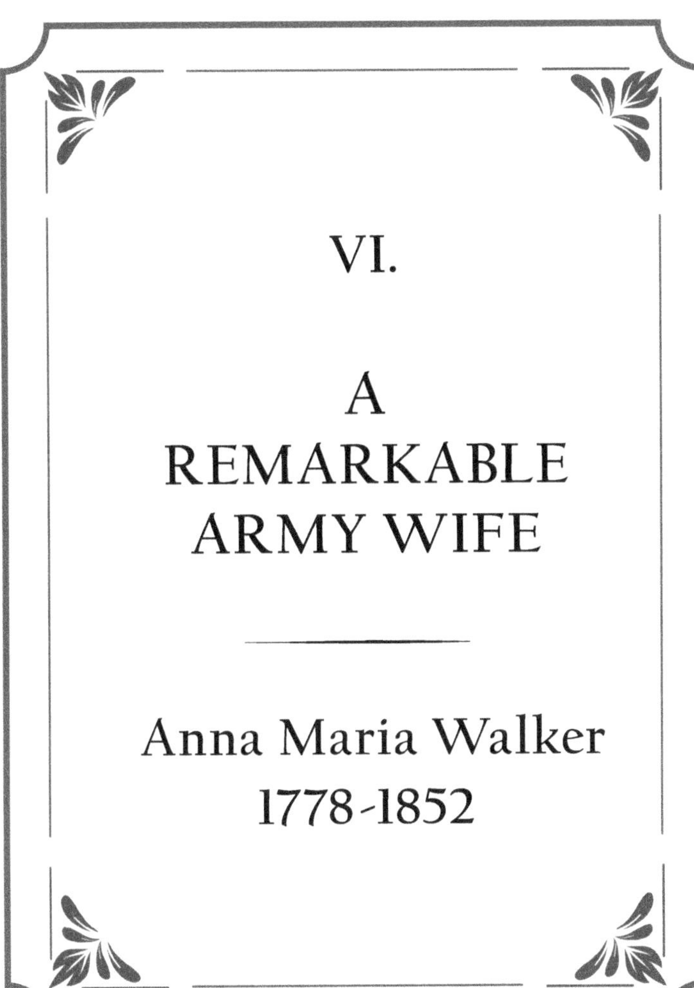

VI.

A REMARKABLE ARMY WIFE

Anna Maria Walker

1778-1852

St Helena by G.H.Bellasis 1815
Courtesy sthelenaisland.info

ANNA MARIA WAS NO STRANGER TO ADVENTURE. At 24, she left Scotland and made the long sea voyage to St. Helena. The infamous pirate naturalist William Dampier had been there. Joseph Banks, homeward bound from Captain Cook's *Endeavour* expedition, stopped in. It was Napoleon's final home. But when Anna Maria and her sisters arrived at the island colony on a stormy morning they found only a very large rock, and water. As Charles Darwin described it, "the island rises abruptly like a huge black castle from the ocean." The closest land mass was Africa, 1200 miles to the west. Brazil lay 1800 miles to the east.

The young ladies struggled ashore carrying what baggage they could manage. Their father stayed behind, arranging delivery of the additional crates and chests to Government House. After many years' service in Bengal, Colonel Robert Patton had been appointed Governor General of St. Helena. The year was 1801.

Slowly the British outpost became home. The Colonel built a promenade for his daughters adjoining Government Garden, still known today as The Sisters Walk. There was a small community of European families on the island, a larger contingent of military personnel, and a slight population of freed slaves.

Passing guests, though, were plentiful. St. Helena was the chief stopping point for European ships replenishing supplies on the journey to the East Indies. It boasted abundant fresh water, food, and a unique ecosystem. The astonishing range of tropical plants caused many a traveller interested in natural history to pause and botanize.

William Roxburgh compiled a flora during his visit. Joseph Burchell, son of the owner of Fulham Nursery in London and a member of the Linnaean Society, arrived with plans to go into trade. Meeting with no success, he became the resident schoolteacher. The Governor quickly added to Burchell's duties: He appointed the young man the island's first Botanist-in-Residence, a position which proved the start of a tremendous career in botany for Burchell.

Lord Valentia passed through with the artist Henry Salt. They botanized, and Anna Maria painted landscapes during the same period, likely in the company of Salt. Lord Valentia returned to England so inspired by the plants of the tropics that he built a private botanical garden. Salt would go on to become a renowned Egyptologist.

Anna Maria was one of seventeen children. Hence Mrs. Patton was reasonably generous with her children and had sent three daughters along to care for the Colonel. One by one the girls married and left. Anna Maria was the last to go, departing St. Helena in 1809 with her new Scottish husband, Col. George Warren Walker. He was in the East India Regiment, and Anna Maria would devote the next 10 years to accompanying him on a series of British campaigns.

Shortly after the Walkers' arrival in India, Anna Maria somehow managed a solo voyage to Ceylon. During that visit she made an historic ascent of Sri Pada, or Adam's Peak, a holy site from ancient times. Texts dating from 400 AD chronicle the Buddha visiting the Peak. In 1298 Marco Polo recorded seeing it in his diaries. Even Sinbad the Sailor of The Arabian Nights visited on his Sixth Voyage.

The morning of Anna Maria's ascent a sea of pilgrims parted. For a foreign female to join the procession was an unprecedented event. She placed a hand on the railing of iron chain and a foot on the first of five thousand stone steps leading to the summit, steps that had been placed in the time of Alexander the Great. At the summit she would find a foot-shaped depression in the rock, claimed by Buddhists to be that of the Buddha. It was said his next footprint as he walked across the Earth on his way to paradise was located in Thailand. Others laid claim to the footprint as well: Hindus recognized it as Shiva's and Muslims identified it as Adam's. When the Portuguese arrived, they claimed it as that of St. Thomas.

Legends of the Peak had it that "From Ceylan to Paradise is forty miles, and the sound of the fountains of Paradise is heard there." A green-clad mini-Matterhorn, it was also called Butterfly Mountain, as during migration season the mountain is carpeted with butterflies. Legend also had it that the watersheds surrounding the Peak were filled with emeralds, rubies and sapphires, a legend based on fact.

Anna Maria would return and climb the peak again with her husband, as Ceylon was to be their home after becoming a British Crown Colony in 1802. Coincidentally that transfer of power from Dutch to British in Ceylon was masterminded by a Scottish neighbour and friend of the

Walkers, Sir Hugh Cleghorn. After completing the negotiations, Sir Hugh smuggled the change of orders into the British garrison past the Dutch, with the papers concealed inside a Dutch Edam cheese!

Sri Pada Summit 1890
Courtesy lankapura.com

Sri Pada Adam's Peak Today
Courtesy ceylonexpeditions.com

The move to Ceylon began a life-changing chapter in the Walkers' life. Ceylon was the home of innumerable plants and in 1810 Joseph Banks proposed building a Botanic Garden there. The British had benefitted tremendously from their botanical efforts in India, both scientifically and commercially, and here was yet another unexplored, unique ecosystem.

The location chosen was a small peninsula in the harbor of Colombo, Slave Island. It was to be called Kew. The botanical wunderkind Alexander Moon, another Scot, was chosen to head the effort, but he found the site rife with problems. In 1817 Moon chose a new location: Peradeniya, where the King of Kandy's gardens had been located for over 500 years.

View Near Point De Galle, Ceylon by Henry Salt 1809
Courtesy British Library

The kingdom of Kandy was located in Ceylon's interior and maintained its autonomy until 1815, when it fell to the British. Here was the island's botanical paradise—a large, uncharted area brimming with plant life. There would be over 188 species of wild orchids identified in Ceylon, and more than half of them grew in Kandy. Moon and the Walkers had the historic honor of being among the first—often *the* first—Europeans to botanize and collect there.

The Walkers were not trained in the natural sciences. While on furlough in Scotland Anna Maria had by mere chance made the acquaintance of William Hooker and Robert Graham who were heading the Botanical Gardens at Glasgow and Edinburgh universities, respectively. In their world, botanical information from the East Indies was invaluable. The botanists enlisted the Walkers to collect and send samples, and were tremendously lucky in their choice.

George stepped into the complex world of plant taxonomy. Anna Maria undertook botanical illustration, complaining in letters to Hooker about her lack of ability. How pleased she would have been to read a later entry in the *India Journal of Agriculture and Botany:* "Previous to 1838, Col and Mrs. Walker paid great attention to Ceylon botany. Mrs. Walker had the advantage of being an excellent flower painter, and her tracings of plants are considered very beautiful."

Acanthepippium bicolor, Anna Maria Walker 1852
Courtesy Royal Botanical Gardens Edinburgh

In reading the Walkers' letters to Hooker, the knowledge and observational skills they brought to identifying plants are astonishing, considering the two were truly "amateurs." They absorbed existing works on the area by Moon, Nathaniel Wallich, and James Wight. They received journals from London like Curtis' *Botanical Journal,* and taxonomic works via Hooker.

Hooker was delighted to provide what support he could to the two, sending a microscope and a plant press along with botany books. Clever man, he was also keenly aware of his great good fortune in having a female correspondent; Anna Maria kept journals of two botanical expeditions, and despite her reservations he published them both in his *Journals of Botany*, one in 1833 and one in 1840. The first journal was a record of Anna Maria's second ascent of Adam's Peak. George accompanied her, and the two engaged in scientific cataloguing of geographic measurement and temperature as well as botanical exploration through Kandy. The second journal recorded a botanical expedition in parts of the island new to the Walkers.

Anna Maria's journals capture the derring-do spirit of botanizing in the tropics. She braves leeches, not as unpleasant as she would have thought: "I had a great dread of them, but experienced no inconvenience from their bite, not even being aware of it until I found myself bleeding profusely in several places."

She sees alligators and albino monkeys. Elephants are an ongoing threat: "We were preceded this morning by our musicians. This custom, though it seems ridiculous to us, has its origin in reason, and expediency—having an opposite effect from the Strains of Orpheus, alarming and scaring away, instead of attracting the 'savage beast'...proving that elephants have a good musical ear and cannot bear the approach of Chinghalese tomtom and pipes, the most discordant of all noises."

Reports of marauding elephants greeted them at one camp, and she learns that the trees in the settlements are filled with platforms for this contingency. At the sound of approaching elephants, the residents take to the platforms with torches, as the elephants flee from the light.

The guesthouses along the way are decorated in preparation for the Walkers' arrival. Garlands of areca-nut flowers, lycopodium and cocoa branches grace the structures. Bowls filled with pineapples, pomegranates, oranges, plantains, melons, coconuts, and honeycomb grace the tables.

There is tremendous range in the nature of the accommodations. Anna Maria is good natured in this regard, but as with others attempting to draw plants and flowers while on tropical expeditions, she is repeatedly foiled by damp, wind, and lack of light.

Her husband usually travels by pony, she by various forms of sedan chair. In one community where no one had ever seen a horse, much less a man upon a horse, George is mistaken for a centaur. Anna Maria describes the design of her favourite variety of sedan chair as a cross between a cradle and a coffin.

Her wit is consistent. Reporting exasperation with curious groups of villagers as she takes her meals, she comments they "doubtless had never witnessed the Knife-and-Fork exercise." She is humble in letting the women have their first close viewing of a non-native woman, remarking she wishes they had a younger example. By the time of the second expedition, she was 59 years old.

She is often awed by the perfect beauty she encounters. At Ramboddwe, an area famous for its waterfalls: "Impatiens and orchideae were the subjects of my pencil. I never saw anything equal to the effects of light and shadow here, every moment bringing some new and beautiful object into view; the falling waters now glancing in the sun-beam, now softened by shade; the glowing tints of the splendid foliage, contrasted with the dark rocks, form altogether a most splendid and varying landscape, far beyond the pencil to portray, or the pen to describe."

On their second expedition Anna Maria marks the Walkers' entry into "terra incognita;" she and the Colonel will be the first foreigners to enter a particular area of the interior. Here she finds the banks of the river adorned with native amaryllis.

They approach Gallegame, and she describes the scenery as "quite enchanting, becoming more and more beautiful every step we proceeded and the variety of plants of all descriptions, trees, shrubs, and flowers, quite endless. I never enjoyed anything more than this day's journey, and only regretted the improbability of my ever travelling over such a delightful route again."

How accurate her sentiment. Change was bearing down on Ceylon quickly. By their second journey, the Walkers encountered denudation of the forests not only for roads, but for coffee and tea plantations. Doubtless not only would Anna Maria never see the pristine area again, few others would as well.

From 1830-36, the Walkers sent over 1700 types of seed to the Royal Botanic Gardens in Edinburgh, as well as hundreds of orchid roots. Anna Maria had clearly outgrown the title of amateur—she alerted the formidable William Hooker to an error he had made in identifying a species of Nepenthes as Ceylonese. *Nepenthes khasiana* was in fact a northeast

India plant, not the *N. distillatoria* of Ceylon, she accurately observed.

Drying and storing plants and seeds for the hostile conditions of a long sea voyage was a tremendous frustration for all plant collectors in the tropics. In the 1830s, Henry Ward debuted his invention, the Wardian Case. A simple terrarium made of glass, it marked a signal moment in the successful shipping of live plant materials throughout the globe. How exciting it must have been to receive the first ingenious glass boxes! In 1837, the Walkers succeeded in delivering live plants to Europe via Wardian Cases for cultivation and classification.

A Wardian Case

In botany, Anna Maria and the Colonel had found their world. On leave in Calcutta they spent a happy 10 days with Nathaniel Wallich who was heading the Calcutta Botanic Gardens. They met Mr. Nightingale, a private collector sent by the Duke of Northumberland to gather orchids. They lamented Wallich's pick for head of the gardens at Peridenya, a Mr. Watson, finding him an unintelligent drunkard; Anna Maria wryly comments: "Watson will be credited with the large collection of plants entitled the Dubiosae."

The botanical giant Robert Wight came to Ceylon during their residency as well. Wight was one of the famous Scottish surgeon-botanists of the era, and the first to attempt a full catalogue of the flora of India. He had headed the Madras Botanic Gardens for several years and attained no small degree of notoriety in botanical circles on arriving in England with his collection of botanical samples in 1831. He had brought home over 200,000 specimens representing over 300 species. His luggage weighed in at 2 tons!

On his return to the East Indies, he and Colonel Walker collected together in Ceylon for six weeks. They returned from the trip with over 500 species. Wight commented that, after showing the Colonel how he collects, he felt Walker would do as much in one year as he had hith-erto done altogether. Shortly after meeting the Walkers, Wight signed on to complete the cataloguing efforts begun by Moon at the Peridenya Gardens. During his 30 years in the East Indies, much of his collecting focused on orchids. Tragically, the hunger for orchids and their subse-quent denudation was attributed to his introductions.

To the end of her life Anna Maria remained in correspondence with William Hooker. In 1851 he was still requesting plant samples from her, that of a palm and a wild pepper. Though George had died some years earlier, he too had been busy with botany until the end. A young man named John George Champion came calling in 1838, requesting the Walkers press Hooker in granting him access to their collection in Edinburgh. One of the new generation of botanist soldiers, Champion took on the role of 'in loco parentis' for the Peradeniya Gardens that the Walkers had filled after Alexander Moon died. The gardens, established in the late 1300s house over 4000 varieties of plants and are visited by over a million Sri Lankans every year.

Anna Maria ended her days at her daughter's compound in Mangalore at the age of 74. The work she and her husband had done on behalf of botany was phenomenal. 78 species of plants were named after them, and over 50 plants collected by them were identified as "new species." How fortunate to have a woman so ready to surpass her expected role in life, to step wholeheartedly into a world she knew nothing of, mastering its many facets alongside her husband and leaving us with a trove of groundbreaking contributions to botany.

Liparis Walkeriae
Curtis Botanical Journal 1840

Vanilla Walkeriae
Jaspe Photos

VII.

AFRICA
and the
LADY SCIENTIST

Sarah Wallis Bowdich Lee
1791-1856

The Gold Stool of the Ashanti
The stool is a royal and divine throne,
said to house the spirit of the nation.
Courtesy blackpast.org

1816 CAME TO BE KNOWN AS THE YEAR WITHOUT A SUMMER. A volcano in Indonesia killed 50,000 people and disrupted global weather patterns, resulting in record low temperatures across Europe for many months. The great Romantic poet Lord Byron fled England that year, as did the great Romantic rogue, Beau Brummel—the first, due to a woman, the second from gambling debts.

It was also the year Sarah Wallis Bowdich left England. She travelled down the Mersey, arrived in Liverpool, and booked passage on a merchant ship bound for Sierra Leone. The reason? "Particular circumstances had made it necessary for me to make a voyage." She was twenty-three years old and accompanied only by her infant daughter Florence. Sierra Leone was not even her intended destination, but as it was that of the only ship bound for Africa, she arranged with the captain to find her own way on to Cape Coast, where her husband was stationed.

Sarah had never been to sea before. Coming aboard with baby and baggage at the Liverpool docks, she made a dramatic entrance: "On going to the cabin for the first time, not knowing my way, we… fell into the store-room beneath. I was caught midway by the tiller, but the poor infant fell to the bottom… I, who in my ignorance could not imagine that a hole of any kind in the floor of a vessel could lead anywhere but into the sea, flew on deck, exclaiming that she was lost!" Happily the first mate found the baby, happily perched on a bale of coffee.

Who was this young woman? Records of Sarah's early life are scarce. We know she came from a well-respected family and received a good education, and that the natural world was her favorite area of study. She was a tomboy as a girl, spending her days with her brothers riding in the countryside. When she was 11, her father lost everything and the family moved to humble quarters in London.

Here she met Thomas Bowdich, a hatmaker's son. His passion, too, was nature, and he would become her husband. The couple's honeymoon consisted of riding over 800 miles on horseback exploring Wales!

When Thomas was offered a position with the African Company of Merchants, he jumped at the opportunity to leave behind the dreary life of trade in London. We know he departed forthwith for his new post, no more. Apparently his young wife was inclined to join him.

**Thomas Edward Bowdich, James Thomson;
engraving after a painting by Wm. Derby 1824**
Courtesy britannica.com

Sarah kept a journal of life at sea, and through it we meet this unusual and adventurous young woman. Baby Florence was adored by all the mates: "She, in her turn, repaid their affection by giving them hers in the most decided manner; and so well did she know them that, when other people came on board, though unable to speak, she would make loud and violent resistance if any but her own five and twenty presumed to touch her," said her mother.

Despite severe seasickness, Sarah was persuaded by the crew to join in fishing for sharks. She hooked the largest—on deck, he nearly covered the length of it! Tasting the smoked meat, she said it reminded her of "some coarse tough goose, which had fed in a salt marsh for twenty years."

The ship approached the coast of Africa, and the sails were coated with red sand from the Sahara, and insects. Anchoring at the Isle de Los, Sarah devoted a day to exploring: "The brilliant lizards, hundreds of birds with the most splendid plumage, flew in every direction… the different character of the foliage, the beauty of the flowers, and the perfume that breathed all around, was so new to me, that I almost doubted if it were real." She ate turtle and turtle eggs, and proclaimed them much more agreeable than shark.

At sea again, mutiny ensued. Hearing a commotion on deck, Sarah scrambled to retrieve her child and found herself near the cook, who was wielding his meat cleaver at one of the mates. "To seize his arm, to snatch the knife out of his hand, and throw it into the sea, was an affair of impulse, not reflection," she says.

The captain of a British brig anchored nearby to investigate the commotion and came aboard to find half the crew in irons. He reinstated order handily by proposing the mutineers exchange places with his men on the war ship. The life of a merchant sailor being far better than that of a soldier, a truce was quickly reached. Sarah removed to the British brig, in light of both her safety and the fact that the ship was bound directly to the Cape Coast.

Sarah made port in what is present-day Ghana accompanied by a pod of sperm whales. The British governor was there to greet her but alas, she was informed that Thomas had set sail for England! He had asked leave to attend to personal business in London. We can only conjecture whether he was guided by the same "particular circumstances" Sarah refers to as the motive for her own journey.

Thomas promptly returned, but to the devastation of both parents, baby Florence was lost to fever in the interim. There was a minimum of time together for the young couple; Thomas and his men were charged to proceed to the African interior directly, to negotiate a peace treaty for trade purposes between the mighty Ashanti kingdom and the African Company of Merchants. Sarah would stay at Cape Coast.

Arriving in the Ashanti kingdom in 1817 was surely a mind-boggling experience for Thomas. After weeks of travel, his party reached Kumasi, the capital of Ashanti. As they approached the palace, "an area of nearly a mile in circumference was crowded with magnificence and novelty. The king, his tributaries, and captains, were resplendent in the distance, surrounded by attendants of every description, fronted by a mass of warriors... The sun was reflected, with a glare scarcely more supportable than the heat, from the massive gold ornaments, which glistened in every direction."

"At least a hundred large umbrellas, or canopies, which could shelter thirty persons, were sprung up and down by the bearers with brilliant effect, being made of scarlet, yellow, and the most showy cloths and silks, and crowned on the top with crescents, pelicans, elephants, barrels, and arms and swords of gold; and the valances (in some of which small looking- glasses were inserted) fantastically scalloped and fringed; from the fronts of some, the proboscis and small teeth of elephants projected, and a few were roofed with leopards' skins, and crowned with various animals naturally stuffed."

The British contingent spent weeks in the capital negotiating with the Ashanti king. Thomas acquitted himself well, stepping in when the leader of his entourage faltered. The king found favor with Thomas and agreed to the treaty.

By the time the Bowdiches reunited at Cape Coast Sarah had fallen under the spell of Africa, as had Thomas. The two were already bound by a thirst for adventure: homeward bound, they agreed to return. They had caught a glimpse of a wonderland of plants, animals and people virtually unknown to the rest of the globe. Together, they committed wholeheartedly to pursue the explorer's life.

The journey home was as lively as Sarah's trip out had been. Aboard a 500-ton freighter, they stopped for a load of timber on the river Gaboon, now known as the Oogué. The natives came in droves to see the white woman, their first. Sarah, too, was curious and joined Thomas on a trip to the inland capital. She noted the birds and flowers along the way in her diary. On arrival they were deposited in the house of the king's brother, whom Sarah deemed both kind and wise. She found him charming and reported that he tolerated her teasing generously. There was much fanfare and celebration on her behalf. Serenaded by an incredibly gifted albino and his harp, she stunned the natives by taking the African harp in her own hands and playing it, to great effect.

While there, she also found reason to fault her own impulses. A native girl who believed the whites to be incarnations of the devil was part of the royal entourage. Sarah was deeply despondent when the girl was taken ill after Sarah, in an effort to tease the girl out of her fears, grabbed her face and forced her to look her in the eye.

Back on board, a narrow escape from a cannibal tribe takes place. A storm ensues; lightning hits and breaks the mast. It is 124 degrees in the shade.

Repairs complete, the ship is loaded and sets sail for England. Within days, it is boarded by a Portuguese pirate ship. In a fantastic turn of luck, the captain of the pirate vessel is sick in bed, so his men merely ransack the stores of the British brig and depart. The travelers make do with next to nothing until they cross paths with ships that are able to share supplies.

On board is a panther, a gift to the Bowdiches from the Ashanti king, as well as an assortment of parrots and "monkies." The panther comes to play an important role in the history of zoology: "The spots on his bright and glossy skin destroyed all the rules established by our naturalists, to enable them to distinguish between the panther and young leopard." The animal is utterly tame, raised a vegetarian, and particularly fond of the scent of lavender water. The Bowdiches ultimately presented him as a gift to the Duchess of York.

Arrived in Europe, imagine the couple disembarking at Penzance: "Our appearance was so grotesque as to raise many conjectures in the town whence we came. Our sudden departure had prevented any arrangement of the toilet, and each of us wore caps made of monkey fur, Mr. Bowdich carried a bag made from the skin of Sai's brother (the panther), and I one of a silver grey monkey; the same fur also decorated other parts of my dress, for the sake of warmth; and to increase our extraordinary costume, Mr. Bowdich had on a pair of the yellow boots of Madeira, and I a large and thick African cloth, which had been my bed the preceding night."

They stop first at friends in Falmouth and are given the best down bed. "It appeared to cause suffocation, and as the bed-side carpet promised us a much better chance of repose, there we took our station for the night. We had slept on mats, not only the whole way home, but for years, and it was months before we could be reconciled to the luxury of English bedding."

Shortly after the Bowdiches' return, Thomas published his journal, *Mission to Ashantee from Cape Coast Castle.* The first section of the book relates the voyage to Ashanti, the Englishmen's time in Kumasi, the negotiations and the return journey to Cape Coast. The second section details the history, laws and customs, climate, architecture, and a complete *Materia Medica* of the kingdom. It was a remarkably thorough and professional account and was very well received. The Bowdiches were eager to do more, and to acquire the knowledge required.

Le Jardin Du Roi before 1636, renamed Le Jardin Des Plantes after the French Revolution
Courtesy Bibliothèque du Muséum National d'Histoire Naturelle

For a scientific education, France was the place. The Jardin des Plantes consisted of gardens, a research center with excellent laboratories, and a museum. England had nothing like it. The term 'scientist' would not be coined until the 1830s, but here the most serious practitioners of all the natural sciences—paleontology, zoology, archaeology and botany—were headquartered.

Sarah and Thomas arrived in 1820. Their intelligence and ability were evident, and they quickly became part of the brilliant circle that comprised the "Hotel Cuvier." The work of Alexander von Humboldt, Lamarck, the botanist de Candolle, and the archaeologist Viver Denon, newly returned from exploring ruins in Egypt with Bonaparte, was all headquartered at the Jardin, under the leadership of Georges Cuvier, the "father of paleontology." The Bowdiches were soon working alongside these men.

Unlike the overwhelming majority of explorers, the couple had neither patron nor personal fortune, but planned to fund their own expeditions. They set about publishing in natural history journals, and Sarah translated natural history works from French to English. In 1821, Sarah published a manual entitled *Taxidermy*, the first of its kind. The work came out anonymously, indicating the limits of gender placed on female endeavors at the time. The book was an unqualified success, going to six editions. Sarah also assembled, abridged and illustrated texts of a number of Cuvier's works on birds, shells and mammals for publication.

The fact that Sarah was a core member of this scientific community is astonishing. Women were not even allowed into the building at the Jardin! Clearly her abilities, both with languages and with the sciences, were extraordinary, and the men of the Jardin had no trouble recognizing the fact. Further, during this period Sarah was elected a member, alongside Thomas, of the Wetterauische Gesellschaft für die Gesamte Naturkunde, a tremendously prestigious natural history research society based in Frankfurt.

After three years in Paris, the Bowdiches were ready for their return to Africa. They had added a girl, Tiedle, and a boy, Hope Smith, to their family in Paris, although Sarah had lost another infant there as well. The four Bowdiches departed for Sierra Leone, with Portugal as the first port of call. They proceeded to Madeira, but the winds were not favorable for continuing on, and an entire year passed before they obtained passage for Africa. While they waited, Sarah gave birth to another girl, Eugenia. Thomas kept a detailed diary of flora and fauna in Madeira, as well as meteorological and geological observations and data.

Sarah's notes show that she, too, continued her scientific inquiries: "What can be more delightful than to see the banana and the violet on the same bank, and the malia azedarach (chinaberry), with its dark shining leaves, raising its summit as high as that of its neighbour, the populus alba." Appreciative of the beauty she encounters, yes. But this description is followed by some intensive botanical inquiry: "I have been somewhat puzzled with the laurels (wanting almost entirely on the continent of Africa), which are so interesting from their uses, their beauty, and the height at which they grow, that I was very desirous of gaining exact information respecting them." This leads into several paragraphs describing

Illustration from *Taxidermy: Or, the Art of Collecting,
Preparing, and Mounting Objects of Natural History
For the Use of Museums and Travelers, 1820* by Sarah Bowdich Lee
Courtesy Whipple Library

her quest: The comparison of Humboldt's literature with that of the old botanical standbys, Persoon and Willdenow, the fine distinctions between four varieties of Madeira laurel, leading into a detailed commentary on how botanical medicines were made by a number of African tribes. She simply was a scientist by nature.

Sarah also loved to laugh. With the family finally at sea, bound for Africa, she is awakened one night by rustling in the cabin. She startles in her bunk and sees a ship's mate dart off, bearing a large knife. Everyone aboard the ship found this particular man very disagreeable, and Sarah reports to Thomas that surely he is a villain and a murderer, and they must be alert for his return in the night. The next night the episode repeats. The sailor passes by the bunks and makes for the locker holding the meat, where he cuts himself off a large chunk and departs. She hopes Thomas has ignored her instructions to stay vigilant, but the sailor's departure is followed by a loud burst of laughter from Thomas. "My imagination carried me to considerable length, to no small entertainment of Mr. Bowdich, and myself also, after I recovered from my fright…"

She also loved a prank, though she is consistently quick to contrition when one goes awry. On an expedition to Cape St Mary's it was necessary on reaching the river to climb a tree, fire a gun to scare off crocodiles, and summon the canoe to take the party across. A lady "new to the wild" was one of their group. Once across, Sarah fell behind her and rustled the bushes, proclaiming that no doubt there was a wild beast nearby. The next day the group learned that shortly after their passing a panther was captured on the very path they had taken! Again, Sarah is crestfallen by her ill-timed high spirits.

Halfway through Thomas' record of this second African journey, the narrative is taken up by Sarah. After locating passage from Madeira south, the family had proceeded to the Gambia, planning to explore there for several weeks en route to Sierra Leone. Thomas began intensive expeditions immediately and contracted a fever. Sarah nursed him around the clock for eight days, to no avail. He died in her arms less than a month after their arrival.

Suddenly alone in Africa with three small children, Sarah booked passage for England. Incredibly, she faced yet more adversity as she claimed her possessions at the dock: "Though disappointed in all other respects, I was returning with a splendid herbarium, carefully packed in a case which seemed impenetrable. The vessel in which I returned was so overladen, and consequently, so deep in the water, that, as we had a succession of storms, from the moment we made the Azores till we reached *Dover*, her deck was incessantly afloat; the water penetrated, and most of my property was destroyed… I can scarcely describe my mortification, at seeing many of my valuable books, maps, and engravings, but above all, my dried plants, drop at my feet in atoms. I was thus disabled from comparing my herbarium with the magnificent collections of England and France, and all I can now do with my new, or imperfect genera, is to offer them as notes for any future traveler."

She continued, "With regard to those which I profess to have determined, I offer them with some degree of confidence, for, since my return, I have re-examined my notes, and the remnants of my specimens, amid the collection in the Jardin du Roi, and have scarcely had a single instance to alter. At the end of each name, I have added the country to which the plant has been hitherto supposed to be indigenous… and I have given the uses made of it by the natives."

Sarah could not afford time for grief. She set to organizing Thomas' notes from the journey for publication. Although kind friends had taken up a collection on her behalf, the gesture was no solution to her lack of resources. Sarah wrote all the addenda for this second volume of Thomas's, doubling its size. She included a formidable appendix of botanical findings, one on their zoological findings, and a narrative continuing the events of the voyage from the time Thomas took ill.

Her introduction to the volume is couched in apology, as was the custom for the female author at the time. And, naturally, great sorrow. It is crystal clear that her reticence belies a depth of knowledge. The continued narrative authored by her includes a trove of information about the plants, animals and customs of the people of West Africa.

Journey to Madeira and Porto Santo was published, and this volume also met with success. But with Thomas gone, Sarah's professional opportunities were dramatically limited, even in the face of her proven ability. Her work in Paris with Cuvier, the "father of paleontology," continued apace. She divided her time between London and Paris. Cuvier's wife and daughter were active participants in his work, and Sarah was a close family friend as well as a welcome and respected colleague.

When Joseph Banks returned from the *Endeavour* expedition, Cuvier sent Sarah to examine Banks' specimens for inclusion in Cuvier's definitive book, *Histoire Naturelle des Poissons*—the only specimens in the entire publication that Cuvier did not personally analyze. Sarah also contributed sketches she had made at St. Jago for the volume. She is acknowledged by Cuvier and his co-author, Valenciennes, in over twenty places in that publication. Sarah would go on to write Cuvier's definitive biography after his death, an honor twice over, as she was neither French nor male.

Sarah began publishing under her own name for the first time after *The Journey to Madeira and Porto Santo* went to print. She was married again in 1826, to a Mr. Lee. Lee was a clerk by profession, but we know little else of him or of their life together.

That year the publisher Rudolf Ackermann asked Sarah to write a story about Africa for inclusion in his literary annual, *Forget Me Not.* He was a friend and she agreed to this departure from publications based on natural history. Ackermann would not let her go and she contributed to the annual for over 20 years. An anthology of her contributions was later published, entitled *Stories of Strange Lands.* The stories are fables set in

Excursions in Madeira and Porto Santo by Sarah Bowdich 1825
Courtesy Abe Books

Africa, and although the stories were indeed a departure from scientific works, Sarah filled each tale with footnotes about the natural world and the customs of West Africa. Further, several of the stories were her own translations of traditional fables from the Persian.

She also began work on the spectacular volume, *Fresh Water Fishes of Great Britain*. Each volume would contain 48 original plates of her meticulously accurate paintings and drawings. She pioneered a technique of using gold and silver foil in the illustrations to replicate the appearance of fish scales. A true masterwork, the book took over ten years to complete. Sarah certainly did not recoup the investment of time and energy, but into the 1950s the work was considered not only a beautiful volume but a valuable scientific resource. There were only fifty copies printed, one of which came to auction in 2001 and sold for $42,000.

Despite having remarried, Sarah continued in straitened circumstances and took every opportunity to publish. She wrote articles regularly for Loudon's *Magazine of Natural History*, several of which were included in the Royal Society's Catalogue of Scientific Papers 1800-1863.

In the 1840s she turned to children's books, one of the few venues where gender was no barrier. Her first two works were educational books

The Freshwater Fishes of Great Britain
Plate 3 by Sarah Bowdich Lee 1828-38
Courtesy Emmanuel College

on botany and natural history. These were followed by novels based on stories about animals, birds, reptiles and fishes.

In a letter to Mary Mitford in 1836, Susanna Moodie, who would become a pioneering traveler herself, visited London and wrote: "I saw but few of the literary lions… Mrs. Lee was the most charming specimen of the female literati to whom I had the honor to be introduced…and this is the same woman whose diaries are filled with hair raising stories about the rats, snakes, spiders and cockroaches of Africa!"

Sarah would not return to Africa. Years later, she wrote: "Why is it, that everyone who has lived in Northwestern Africa… should retain so deep an attachment to that barbarous land? It is not, like other tropical countries, a scene of luxury; on the contrary, it is a life of incessant danger and privation. It possesses not the charm of refined and intellectual society; its European inhabitants, with very few exceptions, professedly try to get money as fast as they can, that they may return to England; and yet when they do return, there is no place on earth so dear to them as the land they have left. And so it is with myself. I have visited other lands, nay, lived in them, and my path has been broken and rugged. Still more thorny was it in Africa, and yet my thoughts and feelings incessantly recur with indescribable affection to those wild scenes; every minute circumstance vividly rushes before me as if it were the occurrence of yesterday, and my very dreams are of that magnificent land, where Nature has lavished her treasures with such unlimited profusion.

"Perhaps these treasures form one of the secret links of that chain which binds us all to her; and her lofty primitive mountains, her mighty rivers, her impenetrable forests, her deep blue sky, where the sun and the moon sail in cloudless majesty, and banish all idea of darkness."

Sarah Eglonton Wallis Bowdich Lee died at her daughter's house in Kent at the age of 65. She had published over twenty books. She is credited with the initial collection and description of six genera, two species of plants, and six species of fish. The spectacular *Bowdichia kunth* tree is named after her and Thomas.

Late in life she was granted a pension from the government based on her achievements and contributions to natural history—yet another in her list of extremely rare achievements for a woman. She was among the handful of women included in Britain's *Dictionary of National Biography.*

Sarah was the first woman to study and write about the plants and animals in the West African interior. Another Englishwoman visited Africa with her husband in the late 1700s and also kept a journal. Here are her notes from an outing: "We were also treated with the perfumes of fragrant aromatic plants, and indeed were vastly delighted and entertained, though I felt fatigued, with our perambulation." Not to put too fine a point on it, but we are reminded once more that Sarah Bowdich Lee was a person at great remove from the average lady of her—and perhaps any—time. The many facets of her life mark her as a remarkable scientist. A true heroine, she bowed to neither the limits of society nor to those of personal tragedy.

Bowdichia Vigilioides Kunth
Courtesy Alex Popovkin

ACKNOWLEDGEMENTS

But for our local library in tiny Ashland, Oregon this book would not exist. I sought refuge there one wintry afternoon when our internet was on the blink at home. I was on deadline for a garden design project and in researching a plant I came across the name of a female plant hunter working in the early 1800s. Soon I was at the library for hours most every afternoon. One name was leading to another, and I was amazed—I had never heard of any of these women!

The reference desk was my refuge. It was staffed by a group of endlessly kind, patient and capable individuals, and through them I spent well over a year ordering in books from around the world. Without the consistently cheerful encouraging presence of Mary, Amy and Ken, this book would not have come to be. How grateful I am for our libraries.

To all of you who took an interest in this project early on, you kept it alive. Deep thanks to each of you: Robin Heald, who told me unequivocally "this book is publishable"; my ace advisor Julie Benezet; Laura Benedetti, beloved gardener and reader who took the time to have the entire document printed in book form; Joan Kreiss, rosarian extraordinaire, whose discerning approval meant the world; Carole Florian, for her generous proofing eye; the wonderful Julie Kierstead who reminded me "plantswomen take care of each other"; Ryan Kirkby, who, whenever our paths crossed, unfailingly asked if I had published the book yet; Sarah Newman, comma queen and so much more; and to Chris Molé: You work that final magic, making an idea into reality.

Two women took the time to exchange ideas with me during early days on the project. Georgina Reid and Jennifer Jewell are true giants in the world of plants and gardens, and the ability to discuss my ideas with you was an honor and a deep source of encouragement and stamina.

When the pandemic hit, it afforded me a rest from querying publishers. Thanks to Ellie Anderson at the Ashland Public Library and Carlotta Lucas, Viki Ashford, and Sheri Morgan at the Ashland Garden Club, I had a chance to tackle Zoom presentations, and thus to hear the audience members ask the logical question: "Where's the book?" Many thanks for that key question, and for withstanding the patience required for early Zoom gatherings.

Finally thank you to my beautiful crazy quilt of a family. Your ongoing encouragement and love over the years make up the nest that brought this book into being. And always foremost, my trailblazer, Jim.

BIBLIOGRAPHY

Alstomer, Clas. *Letters to Linnaeus.*1764-65.

Archer, Mildred, et al. *Treasures from India: The Clive Collection at Powis Castle.* United Kingdom, Meredith Press, 1987.

Arnold, David, *The Tropics and the Traveling Gaze: India, Landscape, and Science, 1800-1856.* United Kingdom, University of Washington Press, 2014.

Baker, Audrey. *The Portland Family and Bulstrode Park,* Buckinghamshire Archaeological Society Archive.

Bell, John. *La Belle Assemblée: Or, Court and Fashionable Magazine; Containing Interesting and Original Literature, and Records of the Beau-monde.* United Kingdom, 1816.

Bennett, Jennifer. *Lilies of the Hearth: The Historical Relationship Between Women & Plants.* United States, Camden House, 1991.

Birkett, Dea. *Off the Beaten Track: Three Centuries of Women Travellers.* London, National Portrait Gallery, 2006.

Blomfield & Inigo. *The Formal Garden in England.* United Kingdom, Macmillian, 1892.

Boddy, Kasia. *Geranium.* United Kingdom, Reaktion Books, 2012.

Bowdich, Thomas Edward, and Lee, R. *Excursions in Madeira and Porto Santo: During the Autumn of 1823, While on His Third Voyage to Africa.* United Kingdom, G.B. Whittaker, 1825.

Bowdich, Thomas Edward. *Essay on the Superstitions, Customs, and Arts Common to the Ancient Egyptians, Abyssinians, and Ashantees.* France, J. Smith, 1821.

Bowdich, Thomas Edward. *Mission from Cape Coast Castle to Ashantee: With a Descriptive Account of that Kingdom.* United Kingdom, Griffith & Farran, 1819.

Breasted J.H. *A History of the Ancient Egyptians.* Scribner, 1908.

Busteed, Henry Elmsley. *Echoes from Old Calcutta: Being Chiefly Reminiscences of the Days of Warren Hastings, Francis and Impey.* India, Thacker, Spink, 1888.

Callcott, Maria. *A Scripture Herbal.* United Kingdom, Longman, Brown, Green, and Longmans, 1842.

Callcott, Maria. *Journal of a Residence in Chile, During the Year 1822: And a Voyage from Chile to Brazil in 1823.* United Kingdom, Longman, Hurst, Rees, Orme, Brown, and Green, and John Murray, 1824.

Callcott, Maria. *Journal of a Voyage to Brazil: And Residence There, During Part of the Years 1821, 1822, 1823.* United Kingdom: Longman, Hurst, Rees, Orme, Brown, and Green, and John Murray 1824.

Chambers. 'Storys of Plants': The Assembling of Mary Capel Somerset's Botanical Collection at Badminton *Journal of the History of Collections* Volume 9, Issue 1, 1997.

Cook, Alexandra. "Botanical Exchange: Jean Jacques Rousseau and the Duchess of Portland" *History of European Ideas* Vol 33, Issue 2, 2007.

Cottegnies, Thompson, Parageau. *Women and Curiosity in Early Modern England and France.* Brill 2016.

County Durham: *Under the Microscope: A look at Lady Anne Monson 'Remarkable Lady Botanist.'* Raby blog.

Creese and Creese. *Ladies in the Laboratory: American and British Women in Science, 1800-1900: A Survey of Their Contributions to Research.* United States, Scarecrow Press, 1998.

Davies, Julie. *Science in an Enchanted World: Philosophy and Witchcraft in the Work of Joseph Glanvill.* Taylor and Francis 2021.

Delany, Mary. *Letters from Mrs. Delany to Mrs. Frances Hamilton, from the year 1779, to the year 1788; comprising many unpublished and interesting anecdotes of their late Majesties and the Royal Family, etc. [With a biographical sketch, and a portrait.].* United Kingdom, Longman, Hurst, Rees, Orme & Brown, 1820.

Delany. *The Autobiography and Correspondence of Mary Granville, Mrs. Delany: With Interesting Reminiscences of King George the Third and Queen Charlotte.* United Kingdom, R. Bentley, 1862.

Dickenson, Mary Hamilton. *Mary Hamilton: Afterwards Mrs. John Dickenson, at Court and at Home. From Letters and Diaries, 1756 to 1816.* United Kingdom, J. Murray, 1925.

Du Plessis, E.P. *Botanical Exploration in South Africa.* Cape Flora: Some of the lectures given on this theme at the University of *Cape Town's Public Summer School.* January-February 1972. University of Cape Town, Board of Extra-Mural Studies, 1972.

Duchess of Portland, Margaret Cavendish Holles Harley Bentinck. *Margaret Cavendish Bentinck, Duchess of Portland Correspondence.* United Kingdom, Electronic Enlightenment Project, 2008.

Durant, Horatia. *Henry, 1st Duke of Beaufort and His Duchess, Mary.* United Kingdom, Hughes & Son, 1973.

Findly, Ellison Banks. *Nur Jahan: Empress of Mughal India.* United Kingdom, Oxford University Press, 1993.

Frankcom, Daniel, et al. *The Duchess of Beaufort's Flowers.* United Kingdom, Webb & Bower, 1983.

Gáldy and Bracken. *Women Patrons and Collectors.* United Kingdom, Cambridge Scholars Pub., 2012.

Gascoigne, John. *Joseph Banks and the English Enlightenment: Useful Knowledge and Polite Culture.* United Kingdom, Cambridge University Press, 2003.

Gates, Barbara T. *Kindred Nature: Victorian and Edwardian Women Embrace the Living World.* University of Chicago Press, 1998.

George and Martin, guest editors "Introduction 'Women and Botany' special issue." *Journal of Literature and Science* Volume 4, Number 1, 2011.

George and Martin. "Mary Somerset and Colonial Botany: Reading between the Ecofeminist Lines." *Modern English Studies Journal* Univ. of Texas Vol 6, 2014.

Graham, Maria. *Journal of a Residence in India.* United Kingdom, Constable, 1813.

Graham, Maria. *The Little Bracken-Burners. A Tale: and Little Mary's Four Saturdays.* United Kingdom, n.p, 1841.

Green, Joseph Reynolds *A History of Botany in the United Kingdom from the Earliest Times to the End of the 19th Century.* J.M. Dent & Sons, limited. 1914.

Greene, Edward Lee. *Landmarks of Botanical History: A Study of Certain Epochs in the Development of the Science of Botany.* United States, Smithsonian Institution, 1910.

Hagglund, Betty. "The Botanical Writings of Maria Graham." *Journal of Literature and Science* Volume 4, No. 1, 2011.

Hahner, ed. *Women Through Women's Eyes; Latin American Women in 19th Century Travel Accounts.* Rowman & Littlefield, 1998.

Heller, Deborah. *Bluestockings Now! The Evolution of a Social Role (British Literature in Context in the Long 18ᵗʰ Century)*. United Kingdom, Taylor & Francis, 2016.

Holmes, Richard. *The Age of Wonder: How the Romantic Generation Discovered the Beauty and Terror of Science*. United States, Knopf Doubleday Publishing Group, 2009.

Hooker, William Jackson. *The Journal of Botany*. United Kingdom, Longman, Rees, Orme, Brown, Green & Longman,1811.

Horwood, Catherine. *Gardening Women: Their Stories From 1600 to the Present*. United Kingdom, Little, Brown Book Group, 2010.

Horwood, Catherine. *Women and Their Gardens: A History from the Elizabethan Era to Today*. United States, Chicago Review Press, Incorporated, 2012.

Irvine. *The Phytologist: A Botanical Journal*. United Kingdom, n.p. 1860.

James Lee *Letters 1776-1806*. The Linnaean Society of London

Jasanoff, Maya. *Edge of Empire: Lives, Culture, and Conquest in the East, 1750-1850*. United Kingdom, Knopf Doubleday Publishing Group, 2007.

Jenkins, Tiffany. *Keeping Their Marbles: How the Treasures of the Past Ended Up in Museums - And Why They Should Stay There*. United Kingdom, OUP Oxford, 2016.

King, Amy. *Bloom: The Botanical Vernacular in the English Novel*. United Kingdom, Oxford University Press, 2003.

Laird & Weisberg-Roberts. *Mrs. Delany & Her Circle*. United Kingdom, Yale Center for British Art, 2009.

Laird, Mark. *The Flowering of the Landscape Garden: English Pleasure Grounds, 1720-1800*. United States, University of Pennsylvania Press, Incorporated, 1999.

Landry, Donna. *The Invention of the Countryside: Hunting, Walking and Ecology in English Literature, 1671–1831*. United Kingdom, Palgrave Macmillan UK, 2001.

Lee, R. *Stories of Strange Lands: And Fragments from the Notes of a Traveller*. United Kingdom, E. Moxon, 1835.

Lee, Sarah. *Elements of Natural History*. United States, Creative Media Partners, LLC, 2016.

McVicker, Mary F. *Women Adventurers, 1750-1900: A Biographical Dictionary, with Excerpts from Selected Travel Writings.* United States, McFarland, Incorporated, Publishers, 2013.

Montagu, Elizabeth Robinson. *Elizabeth Montagu, the Queen of the Bluestockings: Her Correspondence from 1720 to 1761.* United Kingdom, E.P. Dutton, 1906.

Munroe, Jennifer. "'My Innocent Diversion of Gardening': Mary Somerset's Plants." *Renaissance Studies* Vol. 25, No.1, 2011.

Myers, Sylvia Harstark. *The Bluestocking Circle: Women, Friendship, and the Life of the Mind in Eighteenth-century England.* United Kingdom, Clarendon Press, 1990.

Noltie, Henry J. *The Botanical Collections of Colonel and Mrs. Walker: Ceylon, 1830-1838.* Royal Botanic Garden, Edinburgh 2014.

Nordenstam, B. "Carl Peter Thunberg (1743-1828)." *Transactions of the Royal Society of South Africa, 1994,* Vol. 49 (2).

Opitz, Bergwik, Tiggelen, Ed. *Domesticity in the Making of Modern Science.* United Kingdom, Palgrave Macmillan, 2016.

Orr, Mary. *Women Peers in the Scientific Realm: Sarah Bowdich (Lee)'s Expert Collaborations with Georges Cuvier, 1825–33.* Royal Society Publishing, 2014.

Peacock, Molly. *The Paper Garden: Mrs. Delany Begins Her Life's Work at 72.* United States, McClelland & Stewart, 2011.

Pelling, Madeline. "Collecting the World: Female Friendship and Domestic Craft at Bulstrode Park." *Journal for 18th Century Studies* Volume 41, Issue1, March 2018.

Porter, Katherine H. *Margaret, Duchess of Portland.* Cornell University PhD Thesis, 1930.

Quest-Ritson, Charles. *The English Garden: A Social History.* United States, David R. Godine, 2003.

Rauschenberg, Roy, and Joseph Banks. "A Letter of Sir Joseph Banks Describing the Life of Daniel Solander." *Isis* 55, No. 1, University of Chicago Press on behalf of The History of Science Society, 1964.

Read. "Review '*My Innocent Diversion of Gardening: Mary Somerset's Plants.*' by Jennifer Munroe." *Journal of Literature and Science* Volume 4, No. 1, 2011.

Richard H. Grove, *Green Imperialism: Colonial Expansion, Tropical Island Edens and the Origins of Environmentalism, 1600–1860 (Studies in Environmental History)*. Cambridge: Cambridge University Press, 1995.

Samson, Alexander. "Introduction, 'Locus Amoenus': Gardens and Horticulture in the Renaissance." *Renaissance Studies* 25, No. 1, 2011.

Schiebinger, Londa. "Front Matter" *Plants and Empire: Colonial Bioprospecting in the Atlantic World.* Harvard University Press, 2004

Schiebinger, Swan. *Colonial Botany: Science, Commerce, and Politics in the Early Modern World.* University of Pennsylvania Press, 2016.

Shteir, *Cultivating Women, Cultivating Science: Flora's Daughters and Botany in England, 1760 to 1860.* Baltimore: Johns Hopkins University Press, 1996.

Sims, John. "Flower-garden Displayed: In which the Most Ornamental Foreign Plants, Cultivated in the Open Ground, the Green-house, and the Stove, are Accurately Represented in Their Natural Colours." *Curtis's Botanical Magazine*, United Kingdom, n.p. 1833.

Sivasundaram, Sujit. *Islanded: Britain, Sri Lanka, and the Bounds of an Indian Ocean Colony*. India, University of Chicago Press, 2013.

Skeen, William. *Adam's Peak: Legendary, traditional, and historic notices of the Samanala and Sri-Pada: with a descriptive account of the pilgrims' route from Colombo to the Sacred Foot-Print.* WLH Skeen & Co. Ceylon, 1870.

Smith, James Edward. *A Selection of the Correspondence of Vinneus and Other Naturalists from the Original Manuscripts*, 1, n.p. Longman Nurit, 1821.

Strickrodt, Silke. *Those Wild Scenes: Africa in the Travel Writings of Sarah Lee (1791-1856).* Germany, Galda + Wilch, 1998.

Thomson, Thomas. *History of the Royal Society, from Its Institution to the End of the Eighteenth Century.* United Kingdom, Baldwin, 1812.

Thunberg, Carl Peter. Travels at the Cape of Good Hope, 1772-1775. Cape Town*: Van Riebeeck Society,* Series 2, No. 17, 1986.

Todd. *Chrysalis: Maria Sibylla Merian and the Secrets of Metamorphosis.* Harcourt Inc. 2007.

Uglow, Jenny. *A Little History of British Gardening.* United Kingdom, Random House, 2012.

Urban, Sylvanus. *The Gentleman's Magazine, and Historical Chronicle, for the Year 1856*. Vol. 1, London, John Henry and James Parker, 1856.

Vickery, Amanda. *Behind Closed Doors: At Home in Georgian England*. United Kingdom, Yale University Press, 2009.

Vigne, R. "Lady Anne Monson and the Wonders of Cape Flora." *Quarterly Bulletin of the National Library of South Africa*, Vol. 61(2), 2007.

Villiers-Stuart, C. M. *Gardens of the Great Mughals*. London, A. and C. Black, 1913.

Walpole, Horace. *The Duchess of Portland's Museum*. United States, Grolier Club, 1936.

Willes, Margaret. *The Making of the English Gardener: Plants, Books and Inspiration, 1560-1660*. United Kingdom, Yale University Press, 2011.

Withers, Charles W. J., et al. *Travels Into Print: Exploration, Writing, and Publishing with John Murray, 1773-1859*. United Kingdom, University of Chicago Press, 2015.

Wolschke-Bulmahn, Fischer Ed. *Gardens, Knowledge and the Sciences in the Early Modern Period*. Germany, Springer International Publishing, 2016.

Zwaan, Marisca Sikkens-De. "Magdalena Poulle (1632-99): A Dutch Lady in a Circle of Botanical Collectors." *Garden History* Vol. 30, No. 2, 2002.

LUCRETIA WEEMS was trained at U.C.L.A. in the Landscape Architecture program and has been designing gardens in the western United States for over 20 years. She has created landscapes small enough to step across and large enough to get lost in. Researching plants for a design project, she came across the name of a female plant explorer working in the late 1700s. As she found more stories of forgotten women doing important work in the field, she knew those stories had to be told. Lucretia lives, works and gardens in Southern Oregon. This is her first book.

Learn more at www. GardenHistoryHeroines.com